TOP **10**
BOSTON

PATRICIA HARRIS
DAVID LYON
JONATHAN SCHULTZ

EYEWITNESS TRAVEL

Left **Boston Harbor** Center **Massachusetts State House** Right **Ryles**

LONDON, NEW YORK,
MELBOURNE, MUNICH AND DELHI
www.dk.com

Produced by Departure Lounge, London
Printed and bound by South China Printing
Co. Ltd, China
First American Edition, 2003
13 14 15 16 10 9 8 7 6 5 4 3 2

Published in the United States by DK
Publishing, 345 Hudson Street, New York,
New York 10014

**Reprinted with revisions
2005, 2007, 2009, 2011, 2013
Copyright 2003, 2013 © Dorling
Kindersley Limited**

A catalog record for this book is available from
the Library of Congress
ISSN 1479-344X
ISBN 978-0-75669-646-7
Within each Top 10 list in this book, no hierarchy
of quality or popularity is implied. All 10 are, in
the editor's opinion, of roughly equal merit.

MIX
Paper from
responsible sources
FSC™ C018179

Contents

Boston's Top 10

Left **Barking Crab** Center **Store, Newbury Street** Right **Singers, Berklee Performance Center**

Left **Claude Monet's** *La Japonaise,* **Museum of Fine Arts** Right **Memorial Hall**

 Key to abbreviations
Adm *admission charge payable* **Free** *no admission charge* **DA** *disabled access*

3

BOSTON'S
TOP 10

BOSTON'S TOP 10

TOP10 Boston Highlights

"The Hub," "Beantown," "Baaahstin" – call it what you will, New England's largest city exists to be explored. Its colonial-era architecture, vibrant sea-faring heritage, and irrepressible Yankee character make it one of the country's most distinctive locales. Yet for all its big-city amenities – world-class restaurants, museums, and shops – Boston remains surprisingly compact and eminently walkable.

2 Faneuil Hall Marketplace

What was once a dilapidated, post-revolutionary mercantile area now sets the standard for urban-renewal projects worldwide. It boasts an indoor food court in Quincy Market *(left)*, shops, and street performers *(see pp12–13)*.

1 The Freedom Trail

Boston's best walking tour is free, self-guided, chock-full of history, and open year round. Just follow the painted red stripe threading its way past historic buildings such as the Massachusetts State House *(Hall of Flags above; see pp8–11)*.

3 Boston Common & Public Garden

Swan boats drift beneath weeping willows, children splash in fountains, and a bronzed General George Washington *(right)* oversees the proceedings from his lofty steed *(see pp14–15)*.

Charles River

J. J. STORROW MEMORIAL DRIVE
BEACON STREET
Back Bay
COMMONWEALTH
NEWBURY
BOYLSTON
MASSACHUSETTS
5

Fenway

Back Bay Fens

PARK DRIVE
FENWAY
AVENUE
AVENUE
AVENUE
COLUMBUS
TREMONT STREET

8   6
HUNTINGTON

Somerville   Charlestown
4
North End
Cambridge
Downtown
Back Bay
Brookline   Fenway   South End
South Boston

2   miles 0 km   2

4 Harvard University

Boston may have its legendary blue blood, but neighboring Cambridge claims the Harvard Crimson. Pumping vigorously since 1636, the undisputed heart of American academia has cultivated some of the world's greatest thinkers *(see pp16–19)*.

5 Around Newbury Street

Where fashionistas share the sidewalk with punk rockers. Nowhere are the city's myriad fashions *(left)*, faces, and fortunes on more vibrant display *(see pp20–21)*.

Sign up for DK's email newsletter on traveldk.com

6 Museum of Fine Arts, Boston

The MFA, Boston's queen of the visual arts scene, boasts some of the most extensive collections of Japanese, ancient Egyptian, and Impressionist works of art in the world. Van Gogh's *Houses at Auvers* (1890; *left*) is just one of many treasures in the European Art collection *(see pp22–5)*.

7 Trinity Church

This Neo-Romanesque church is regarded as the finest execution of architect H. H. Richardson's distinctive style. Equally impressive is La Farge's stunning *Christ in Majesty* window *(above; see pp26–7)*.

8 Isabella Stewart Gardner Museum

The works of Rembrandt, Botticelli, and Sargent appear all the more masterful in Isabella Stewart Gardner's Venetian-style palazzo. The courtyard's *(left)* myriad treasures include an ancient Roman marble sarchophagus dating to AD 222 *(see pp28–9)*.

9 Charlestown Navy Yard

Boston's deep harbor made it ideal for one of the US Navy's first shipyards. USS *Constitution* *(below)*, the most famous of the yard's progeny, is still docked here *(see pp30–31)*.

10 New England Aquarium

Get personal with three species of penguins, harbor seals, and many other creatures of the deep. The vast 200,000 gallon (900,000 liter) Giant Ocean Tank *(right)* is the aquarium's centerpiece, where an upward-spiraling walkway guides you around the ecosytem *(see pp32–3)*.

🔟 The Freedom Trail

Snaking through 2.5 miles (4 km) of city streets, the Freedom Trail creates a living link to Boston's key revolutionary and colonial-era sites. Stroll from highlight to highlight and you'll see history adopt a vibrancy, palpability, and relevance unparalleled among US cities. Some of Boston's most unique shops, restaurants, and attractions are also located along the trail.

Freedom Trail plaque

⭕ Give your sweet tooth a workout at Mike's Pastry *(see p94).*

⭕ Maps of the trail are available at the Boston Common Visitors' Center. Two-hour MP3 tours cost $15.

Most of the trail is indicated in red paint with a few sections in red brick.

• Start point: Boston Common. "T" station: Park St (red/green lines)
• Finish point: Charlestown. "T" station: Community College (orange line)
• Map: P4 (start)
• www.thefreedom trail.org
• Copp's Hill Burying Ground: Snow Hill St; 617 635 4505; open 9am–5pm daily; free
• Park Street Church: 1 Park St; 617 523 3383
• www.parkstreet.org

Top 10 Features

1. Massachusetts State House
2. Park Street Church
3. Old Granary Burying Ground
4. King's Chapel
5. Old South Meeting House
6. Old State House
7. Faneuil Hall & Quincy Market
8. Paul Revere House
9. Old North Church
10. Copp's Hill Burying Ground

1 Massachusetts State House
Arguably Charles Bulfinch's *pièce de résistance*, the "new" State House (completed in 1798; *above*) is one of the city's most distinctive buildings *(see pp11 & 75).*

2 Park Street Church
Founded by a small group of Christians disenchanted with their Unitarian-leaning congregation, Park Street Church *(above)* was constructed in 1809.

3 Old Granary Burying Ground
A veritable who's-who of revolutionary history fertilizes this plot *(above)* next to Park Street Church. One of its most venerable residents is revolutionary Samuel Adams *(see p38).*

150 ⸺ yards ⌐ 0 ⌐ meters ⸺ 150

Key

—	Freedom Trail
Ⓣ	"T" Station
❶	Tourist Information

4 King's Chapel
The current granite building was erected in 1749, although the chapel was originally founded in 1686 by King James II as an outpost of the Anglican Church. Don't miss the atmospheric burying ground next door, which shelters colonial Governor John Winthrop *(see p98).*

For more information on these areas see chapters on Beacon Hill and Downtown & the Financial District **See pp74–9 & pp96–103**

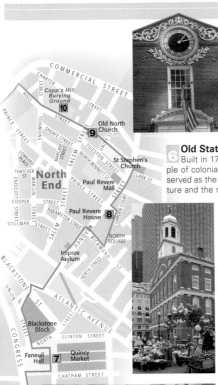

5 Old South Meeting House

What Berkeley's University of California was to the 1960s, Boston's Old South Meeting House was to the colonial era: a crucible for free-speech debates and taxation protests *(see p98)*.

6 Old State House

Built in 1713, this exquisite example of colonial architecture *(above)* served as the HQ of the colonial legislature and the royal governor *(see p97)*.

7 Faneuil Hall & Quincy Market

Known as the "Cradle of Liberty", Faneuil Hall *(left)* has hosted many revolutionary meetings in its time. Neighboring Quincy Market, built in the early 1800s, once housed Boston's wholesale food distribution *(see p12–13)*.

8 Paul Revere House

Nestled in North Square, the Paul Revere House is Boston's oldest private residence. Its principal owner was well regarded locally as a metalsmith prior to his fateful ride *(see p91)*.

An Hour of Freedom

For visitors tight on time, consider this condensed trail. Head up Tremont Street from Park Street "T" station, stopping in the Old Granary Burying Ground. At the corner of Tremont and School streets – site of King's Chapel – turn right onto School and continue to Washington Street and the Old South Meeting House. Turn left on Washington to the Old State House then finish up at Faneuil Hall nearby on Congress Street.

9 Old North Church

This church *(above)* occupies a pivotal place in revolutionary history. Prior to his midnight ride, Revere *(see p38)* ordered sexton Robert Newman to hang lanterns in the belfry, to indicate whether the British were approaching via the Charles River or by land *(see p91)*.

10 Copp's Hill Burying Ground

With headstones dating from the 17th century *(left)*, Copp's Hill is a must for history buffs. It was named after William Copp, a farmer who sold the land to the church *(see p91)*.

Note: From Copp's Hill Burying Ground, the Freedom Trail continues across Charlestown Bridge to Charlestown Navy Yard See pp30–31

Left **Bunker Hill** Center **Statue of Paul Revere** Right **Reenactment of the Boston Tea Party**

🔟 Moments in Revolutionary History

1 Resistance to the Stamp Act (1765)
The king imposed a stamp duty on all published materials in the colonies, including newspapers. Furious Bostonians boycotted English goods in response.

2 Boston Massacre (1770)
Angry colonists picked a fight with British troops in front of the Old State House, resulting in the deaths of five unarmed Bostonians.

3 Samuel Adams' Tea Tax Speech (1773)
Adams' incendiary speech during a forum at the Old South Meeting House inspired the Boston Tea Party, the most subversive action undertaken yet in the debate over colonial secession.

4 Boston Tea Party (1773)
Led by Samuel Adams, the Sons of Liberty protested against the king's tax policy on tea by boarding three British East India Company ships and dumping their cargo into Boston Harbor, a watershed moment of colonial defiance.

5 Paul Revere's Ride (1775)
Revere rode to Lexington to warn revolutionaries Samuel Adams and John Hancock that British troops intended to arrest them. One of the bravest acts of the war, it would be immortalized in the Longfellow poem *The Midnight Ride of Paul Revere*.

6 Battle of Lexington (1775)
Revere's ride was followed by the first exchange of fire between the ragtag colonist army and the British at Lexington.

7 Battle of Bunker Hill (1775)
The colonists' fortification of Charlestown resulted in a full-scale British attack. Although defeated, the colonists' resolve was galvanized by this battle.

George Washington

8 Washington Takes Command (1776)
The Virginia gentleman farmer, George Washington, led the newly-formed Continental Army south from Cambridge to face British troops in New York.

9 Fortification of Dorchester Heights (1776)
Fortifying the mouth of Boston harbor with captured cannon, Washington put the Royal Navy under his guns and forced a British retreat from the city.

10 Declaration of Independence (1776)
On July 4, the colonies rejected all allegiance to the British Crown. Independence was declared from the Royal Governor's headquarters, known today as the Old State House.

For more information on Boston's history and figures in Boston history See pp36–9

Top 10 State House Features

1 23-carat gold dome
2 Senate Chamber
3 House of Representatives
4 "Hear Us" Exhibit
5 Stained Glass Windows
6 Doric Hall
7 Hall of Flags
8 Nurses Hall
9 Sacred Cod
10 State House Pine Cone

The Sacred Cod

Bestowed on the House of Representatives by Boston merchant, Jonathan Rowe, the carving of the Sacred Cod has presided over the Commonwealth's legislative activities since 1784. It disappeared briefly in 1933, when Harvard's *Lampoon* magazine orchestrated a dastardly "codnapping" prank.

Massachusetts State House

The 1798 Massachusetts State House is Charles Bulfinch's masterwork, and among the nation's most mimicked – not to mention earliest – examples of public architecture. With its brash design details, imposing stature, and liberal use of fine materials, the State House embodies the optimism that ran through post-revolutionary America. The building is best understood in three distinct sections: the original Bulfinch front; the marble wings constructed in 1917; and the yellow-brick 1895 addition, known as the Brigham Extension after the architect who designed it. Just below Bulfinch's central colonnade, statues of famous Massachusetts figures strike poses. Among them are the great orator, Daniel Webster, President J. F. Kennedy, and Quaker Mary Dyer, who was hanged in 1660 for challenging the authority of Boston's religious leaders. Directly below the State House's immense gilded dome is the Senate Chamber, which has hosted some of the most influential debates and speeches in US history. The government's larger legislature, the House of Representatives, convenes in the Brigham Extension. While the building's principal purpose remains governmental, the State House also functions as a working museum, boasting important murals, statues, and artifacts from Massachusetts history (see p75).

Massachusetts State House

Faneuil Hall Marketplace

Bostonians may bemoan its popularity with tourists, but this market complex deserves all the attention and accolades it has received since its revitalization in the mid-1970s. Once the pulsing center of Boston mercantile activity, the area fell into disrepair in the 1930s. Today, however, millions of visitors are testimony to its newfound vitality as a shopping and dining destination.

Exterior, Quincy Market

🥣 The soup crocks at Boston Chowda Co in Quincy Market are brimming with piping-hot seafood and veggie chowders.

🎧 The National Park Service conducts free historical lectures in Faneuil Hall's Great Hall every half hour from 9am–4:30pm.

Purchase discounted day-of-performance theater tickets at the BosTix kiosk on Faneuil Hall's south side. Open 10am–6pm Tue–Sat, 11am–4pm Sun.

• Map: Q2
• "T" station: Government Center (green/blue line)
• 617 523 1300 • Great Hall, Faneuil Hall: open 9am–5pm daily; free
• Museum of the Ancient & Honorable Artillery Company: Faneuil Hall; 617 227 1638; open 9am–3pm Mon–Fri; free • Quincy Market: open 10am–9pm Mon–Sat (to 6pm Mon–Thu in winter), 11am–6pm Sun • NPS Visitor Center: open 9am–5pm daily

Top 10 Attractions
1. Quincy Market
2. Faneuil Hall
3. Museum of the Ancient & Honorable Artillery Company
4. Pushcart Vendors
5. North & South Markets
6. Blackstone Block
7. Haymarket Square
8. Samuel Adams Statue
9. Holocaust Memorial
10. Boston Stone

Faneuil Hall
Peter Faneuil, an influential French Huguenot merchant, donated the hall *(below)* to Boston in 1742. The second floor is dominated by the Great Hall, where town meetings once took place. The building also houses the National Parks Visitor Center.

Quincy Market
Quincy Market functioned from 1825 to the 1960s as the city's wholesale food distribution center. By the 1980s, the market had been revived, the grand atrium *(below)* restored, and a food court opened.

Museum of the Ancient & Honorable Artillery Company
Assembled in 1638 to defend the Massachusetts Bay Colony, the company has held court on Faneuil Hall's fourth floor since 1746. The museum boasts war memorabilia dating from the Revolution to the War on Terrorism.

Pushcart Vendors
A "fleet" of more than 40 pushcart vendors is scattered throughout the marketplace and tempts visitors with a delightfully eclectic, often eccentric, array of merchandise from T-shirts to jewelry made by local artisans.

Faneuil Hall and Quincy Market are both sights on the Freedom Trail See pp8–11

North & South Markets

Flanking each side of Quincy Market, these revitalized brick warehouses *(left)* are filled with name-brand shops and many unique restaurants.

Around Faneuil Hall

Blackstone Block

Bounded by Congress, Hanover, Blackstone, and North streets, this block is as old world as Boston gets. The city's first commercial district, named after Boston's first settler, William Blaxton, took root here during the 17th century. Two of the country's oldest dining and drinking establishments – the Union Oyster House and Green Dragon Tavern – call the block home.

Haymarket Square

Friday afternoon and all day Saturday, vendors *(below)* hawk the day's bounty with abandon. Yet for all its boisterous chaos, the Haymarket handsomely rewards with cheap, fresh produce.

Samuel Adams Statue

The city's favorite brewer and patriot is immortalized in front of Faneuil Hall, where he delivered some of the Revolutionary era's most impassioned speeches *(see p10)*. Local sculptor Anne Whitney was commissioned to design the statue in 1880.

Holocaust Memorial

This 1995 memorial *(below)* comprises six glass columns, symbolizing the Nazis' principal death camps. Each column bears the numbers of one million victims, evoking the six million lives destroyed under Hitler.

Boston Stone

Some claim this curious landmark was once the measuring point from which all distances to and from Boston were calculated. The stone is embedded into a brick wall at the corner of Marshall Street and Salt Lane.

True Irish Pubs

The Quincy Market area boasts a bevy of Irish-style pubs. But if you're craving authentic Gaelic atmosphere to complement your black and tan, the choice is more limited than appearances might suggest. Two pubs that make the grade are Kinsale (2 Center Plaza) and the Black Rose (160 State St – both located within two blocks of the marketplace.

Boston Common & Public Garden

Verdant Boston Common has hosted auctions, cattle grazing, and public hangings over its 350-year history, in addition to festivals and the requisite frisbee tosses. The adjacent Public Garden, opened in 1839, was the USA's first botanical garden. Its swan boats, weeping willows, and bridge are emblematic of Boston at its most enchanting. The French-style flowerbeds (center) may only bloom in warmer months, but the garden exudes old-world charm year round.

Sign for Boston Common

🍴 Quick, food court-style bites can be had inside the Corner shopping center, at Washington and Summer streets.

🎭 The Commonwealth Shakespeare Company stages free performances during summer. Contact 617 426 0863 or *www. commshakes.org*

• Bounded by: Beacon, Park, Tremont, Arlington, & Boylston streets
• Map: M4, N4
• "T" station: Park Street (red/green line), Boylston, & Arlington stops (both green line).
• open 24 hours
• Boston Common Visitors' Center: 148 Tremont St; 617 426 3115; open 8:30am–5pm Mon-Fri, 9am–5pm Sat & Sun
• Boston Parks & Recreation: 617 635 4505; www.bostonusa. com • Swan boat rides: 617 522 1966; mid-Apr-mid-Sep: usually 10am–5pm daily; Adm: $2.75; www.swanboats.com

Top 10 Attractions

1. Shaw Memorial
2. Soldiers & Sailors Monument
3. Frog Pond
4. Parkman Bandstand
5. *Make Way for Ducklings* Statuettes
6. Founders' Memorial
7. Lagoon Bridge
8. Swan Boats
9. Bronze of George Washington
10. Ether Monument

Shaw Memorial
Augustus Saint-Gaudens' lifelike bronze pays homage to the "Fighting 54th" – one of the only entirely African-American regiments in the Civil War. Led by Boston native Robert Shaw, the 54th amassed an impressive battle record.

Soldiers & Sailors Monument
Over 25,000 Union Army veterans remembered their fallen Civil War comrades at the 1877 dedication of Martin Milmore's impressive memorial. Bas-reliefs (above) depict the soldiers' and sailors' departure to and return from war.

Frog Pond
During summer, children splash under the iridescent spray of the pond's fountains. Come winter, kids of all ages lace up their skates and take to the ice. Skate rentals and hot chocolate are available at the nearby hut.

Parkman Bandstand
Built in 1912 to honor George Parkman, a benefactor of the park, the bandstand (right) is modeled after Versailles' *Temple d'Amour*. In summer it hosts everything from concerts to graduations.

For sights and attractions in neighboring Beacon Hill
See pp74–9

5 Make Way for Ducklings Statuettes

Eight duckling statues have sprung from the pages of Robert McCloskey's kids' book and fallen in line behind their mother at the lagoon's edge.

6 Founders' Memorial

William Blaxton, Boston's first white settler, is depicted greeting John Winthrop *(see p38)* in John F Paramino's 1930 bronze. Note the word "Shawmut" – the Native American name for the land that would become Boston.

Plan of Boston Common & Public Garden

7 Lagoon Bridge

This elegant 1869 span over the lagoon is often mistaken for a suspension bridge, a tribute to the architect's clever design. It is a favorite spot for wedding pictures.

8 Swan Boats

Summer hasn't officially arrived in Boston until the swan boats emerge from hibernation and glide onto the Public Garden pond. With their gracefully arching necks and brilliantly painted bills, each distinctive swan boat can accommodate up to 20 people.

Emerald Necklace

Boston Common and Public Garden may seem like solitary urban oases, but they are two links in a greater chain of green space that stretches all the way through Boston to the suburb of Roxbury. The Emerald Necklace, as this chain is called, was completed in 1896 by Frederick Law Olmsted, the man behind New York's Central Park.

9 Bronze of George Washington

The nation's first president cuts a stately figure at the western end of the Public Garden. Thomas Ball's 1869 bronze was the first to depict George Washington astride a horse.

10 Ether Monument

This 1868 statue commemorates the first etherized operation, which took place at Massachusetts General Hospital in 1846. Controversial from the outset, this is the West's only monument to the powers of a drug.

For sights and attractions in neighboring Downtown & the Financial District **See pp96–103**

🔟 Harvard University

America's most prestigious university – named in honor of its principal bene-factor, John Harvard, in 1638 – has nurtured, tortured, and tickled some of the greatest minds of the past 350 years. It has hosted everything from global economic summits to kool-aid acid tests, and educated everyone from future US presidents to late-night talk-show hosts. Visitors craving contact with the Harvard mystique are in luck, since much of the university is open to the public.

Memorial Hall

🖥 Students refuel at the Harvard Coop bookstore café (1400 Massachusetts Ave, 617 499 2000).

🎬 Harvard Film Archive, Carpenter Center, screens art and documentary films most nights (Quincy St, 617 495 4700).

Pick up a copy of the student-run newspaper *The Crimson* to see what issues are exercising some of the world's greatest minds.

• "T" station: Harvard (red line)
• www.harvard.edu/ museums;
www.cambridge-usa.org
• Harry Widener Memorial Library: Harvard Yard; 617 495 2411; access only with someone with valid Harvard ID
• Maps and tours available from Holyoke Center: 1350 Massachusetts Ave; 617 495 1573

Top 10 Features

1. Massachusetts Hall
2. John Harvard Statue
3. Memorial Hall
4. Harvard Yard
5. Harry Widener Memorial Library
6. Museum of Natural History
7. Fogg Museum
8. Busch-Reisinger Museum
9. Sackler Museum
10. Peabody Museum of Archaeology & Ethnology

Massachusetts Hall
The university's oldest building, constructed in 1720, acted as a meeting place for revolutionary soldiers. It continues to be a focal point of resistance movements, most recently in 2001, when students occupied the hall's administrative offices in an effort to secure a fair wage for the university's employees.

John Harvard Statue
The statue's *(right)* inscription "John Harvard, Founder 1638" conceals three deceptions, hence its nickname "The Statue of Three Lies". First, there is no known portrait of John Harvard, so the sculptor, Daniel French, used a model; second, John Harvard did not found the university – rather it was named after him; and last, the university was not founded in 1638, but in 1636.

Memorial Hall
Built over 14 years, Harvard's memorial to its fallen union army alumni was officially opened in 1878. Conceived as a multipurpose building, it has hosted graduation exercises, theatrical performances, and assemblies of all kinds.

Harvard Yard
Harvard's mixed residential and academic yard *(left)* became the standard by which most American institutions of higher learning modeled their campuses.

For more on Harvard University and Harvard's museums
See p119

5 Harry Widener Memorial Library

The Widener *(left)* is the largest university library in the US. It houses a special collection of rare books, including a Gutenberg bible and early editions of Shakespeare's collected works.

6 Museum of Natural History

Never mind George Washington's taxidermied pheasants, the enormous Brazilian amethyst geode, or the world's only mounted Kronosaurus skeleton. Check out the glass flowers: 830 species of plants, painstakingly replicated in brilliant, colorful glass.

7 Fogg Museum

During renovation of its building *(left)*, until fall 2014, highlights of the Fogg's collection of Western art from the Middle Ages to the present, including Impressionist works, will be on display at the Sackler Museum.

Museum of Natural History **6**
10 Peabody Museum of Archaeology & Ethnology
OXFORD
D'ANTHY AVENUE
FRISBIE PLACE
KIRKLAND ST
STREET
QUINCY ST
Memorial Hall **3**
CAMBRIDGE STREET
Sackler Museum **9**
HARVARD YARD **4**
Fogg Museum **7**
BROADWAY
PRESCOTT STREET
QUINCY STREET
Busch-Reisinger Museum **8**
5 Harry Widener Memorial Library
AVENUE
QUINCY SQUARE

8 Busch-Reisinger Museum

This museum shares space with the Fogg Museum and will also be closed until 2014. Selections of its German expressionism and Bauhaus-related exhibits will be on display at the Sackler Museum.

9 Sackler Museum

Until 2014, the Sackler *(above right)* will display some of the best pieces from the Busch-Reisinger and the Fogg museums, as well as continuing to exhibit works from its own collections of Asian *(left)*, Egyptian, Islamic, and Indian art.

10 Peabody Museum of Archaeology & Ethnology

Housing one of the world's most comprehensive records of human cultural history, the Peabody caters for the Indiana Jones in all of us. Highlights include The Hall of the North American Indian, a permanent Mesoamerica exhibit, and a gallery devoted to frequently rotating temporary exhibits.

Harvard Lampoon

Lampooners have made you laugh more than you might ever know. Aside from *The Harvard Lampoon* proper being the world's oldest humor magazine, nearly every successful contemporary American comedy to reach a TV or movie screen boasts an ex-Lampooner on its writing staff. One well known ex-Lampooner is Conan O'Brien of *The Simpsons* fame.

Left **Leonard Bernstein** Right **T. S. Eliot**

Harvard Alumni

1 John Adams (1735–1826)
The nation's second president, although nervous upon entering the illustrious college as a freshman, eventually became enthralled by his studies.

2 Franklin Delano Roosevelt (1882–1945)
Apparently more of a social butterfly than dedicated academic, F.D.R. played pranks, led the freshman football squad, and earned a C average at Harvard before he became the 32nd president of the US.

3 W. E. B. Du Bois (1868–1963)
Founder of the National Association for the Advancement of Colored People (NAACP), Du Bois studied philosophy, and said of his experience, "I was in Harvard, but not of it".

4 Oliver Wendell Holmes (1809–94)
The 1861 grad and future Supreme Court Justice was also the class poet, delivering a stirring reading of original work at his Class Day exercises.

5 Al Gore (1924–)
After serving as Vice President under Bill Clinton, Gore lost the 2000 presidential election to George W. Bush. In 2007 he won the Nobel Peace Prize and an Oscar for his film *An Inconvenient Truth.*

6 Leonard Bernstein (1918–90)
The country's greatest composer and conductor was firmly grounded in the arts at Harvard. He edited the *Advocate* – the college's estimable literary and performing arts journal.

John Adams

7 T. S. Eliot (1885–1965)
The modernist poet of *The Waste Land* fame contributed much of his early work to the *Advocate*. He went on to edit many of those submissions for later publication.

8 Henry Kissinger (1923–)
The International Affairs and Government professor, who graduated from Harvard summa cum laude, became President Nixon's National Security Advisor in 1969 and Secretary of State in 1973.

9 Benazir Bhutto (1953–2007)
This class of 1973 alumna later became the first woman to lead a modern Muslim state when she was elected prime minister of Pakistan in 1988. She was assassinated in 2007.

10 Henry James (1843–1916)
The master of the psychological novel sourced plenty of material at Harvard for his scathing 1886 work, *The Bostonians.*

Harvard's Top 10 Buildings

Harvard's "Architectural Zoo"

Prominent modernist architect James Stirling described Harvard as an "architectural zoo" – and with a campus as aesthetically diverse as Harvard's, it's a well-deserved moniker. Stirling was himself responsible for the university's modernist Sackler Museum (see pp17 & 119) opened in 1985. The seemingly ubiquitous architect Charles Bulfinch, whose claim to fame is the Massachusetts State House (see p11), left his mark on Harvard Yard with his 1814 University Hall, featuring an ingenious granite staircase that "floats" – supported solely by virtue of its interlocking steps. In complete contrast Walter Gropius, whose strongly linear residential buildings pepper college campuses throughout the northeast US, contributed the Harvard Graduate Center in 1950. Gropius strove to make his industry-informed projects seem welcoming for their inhabitants, but by most Harvard grad students' accounts, the austere-looking center doesn't exactly scream "Home Sweet Home." One of Harvard's more whimsical buildings is Le Corbusier's Carpenter Center. A wondrous collection of forms and materials, the center boasts entire walls made of glass and deeply grooved concrete. Surprisingly it is Le Corbusier's only design in North America.

Sever Hall

Trinity Church (see pp26–7) architect and 1859 Harvard alumnus H. H. Richardson designed Sever (right) and Austin halls. Both halls echo Richardson's distinctive Romanesque style found on his Copley Square masterpiece

Carpenter Center

TOP10 Around Newbury Street

Don't let the profusion of Prada-clad shoppers fool you: there's more to Newbury Street than world-class retail, people watching, and al fresco dining. One of the first streets created on the marshland known as Back Bay, Newbury has seen a myriad of tenants and uses over the past 150 years. Look closely and you'll glimpse a historical side to Newbury Street all but unseen by the fashionistas.

Newbury Street

⬤ Stock up at Deluca's Back Bay Market (239 Newbury St) and have a picnic.

⬤ View the schedule for Emmanuel Music, a highly respected chamber music society, at www. emmanuelmusic.org or call 617 536 3356.

• Map K5, L5, M5
• "T" station: Arlington, Copley, or Hynes/ICA
• Boston Architectural College: 320 Newbury St; 617 262 5000; open 8:30am–10pm Mon–Thu, 9am–9pm Fri, 9am–5pm Sat, noon–7pm Sun
• Church of the Covenant: 67 Newbury St • Emmanuel Church: 15 Newbury St • French Cultural Center: 53 Marlborough St; 617 912 0400; open 10am–5pm Mon–Thu & Sat; later hours some evenings
• New England Historic Genealogical Society: 101 Newbury St; 617 536 5740; open 9am–5pm Tue–Sat (until 9pm Wed)
• Society of Arts & Crafts: 175 Newbury St; 617 266 1810; open 10am–6pm Tue–Sat
• Trinity Church Rectory, 233 Clarendon St; closed to the public

Top 10 Sights

1 Emmanuel Church
2 Commonwealth Avenue
3 Church of the Covenant
4 Society of Arts & Crafts
5 Boston Architectural College
6 234 Berkeley St
7 Gibson House Museum
8 French Cultural Center
9 New England Historic Genealogical Society
10 Trinity Church Rectory

Commonwealth Avenue
A mall *(above)* running along the center of Commonwealth Avenue provides a leafy respite from the Newbury Street throngs. Benches and historical sculptures line the pedestrian path, where couples and a dog or two stake out their favorite spots.

Church of the Covenant
Although far more famous for his Trinity Church in New York, English-born architect Richard Upjohn also left his Neo-Gothic mark on Boston with the Church of the Covenant *(left)*, erected in 1865.

Emmanuel Church
Architect Alexander Estey's impressive church (1860) was the first building to grace Newbury after the infilling of Back Bay. The adjacent Lindsey Chapel *(1924: right)* is home to the renowned Emmanuel Music.

For more sights and attractions in Back Bay See pp80–83

4 Society of Arts & Crafts
Formed in 1897, the Boston Society of Arts and Crafts was one of the earliest of its kind. Societies such as this helped to elevate the status of traditional arts *(see p84).*

Charles River Basin

Around Newbury Street

5 Boston Architectural College
For more than 100 years, aspiring architects have sought the counsel and workshops offered by the venerable BAC. The McCormick Gallery displays architectural plans and designs.

6 234 Berkeley St
Originally a natural history museum opened in 1864, this landmark building is now undergoing redevelopment as a high-end home goods store.

7 Gibson House Museum
One of Back Bay's first private residences, Gibson House *(above)* was also one of the most modern houses of its day. Boasting gas lighting, indoor plumbing, and heating, it spurred a building boom in the area *(see p93).*

8 French Cultural Center
Housed in a grand Back Bay mansion, the French Cultural Center hosts everything from lectures in French to concerts and a tasteful Bastille Day celebration. The lobby posts wire-service news reports from France.

9 New England Historic Genealogical Society
Members seek to make contact with their New England progenitors in one of the most extensive genealogical libraries in the US. For a fee, you too can try your luck.

10 Trinity Church Rectory
H. H. Richardson, Trinity Church's principal architect, was commissioned to build this rectory *(left)* in 1879. His handiwork reflects the Romanesque style of his Copley Square masterpiece *(see pp26–7).*

Back Bay's Origins

Since its settlement by Westerners, Boston has been nipped, tucked, and reshaped to suit the needs of its inhabitants. Back Bay derives its name from the tidal swampland on which the neighborhood now stands. During the 19th century, gravel was used to fill the marsh and create the foundations for the grand avenues and picturesque brownstones that now distinguish this highly sought-after area.

For more on Newbury Street shopping **See pp85–6**

10 Museum of Fine Arts, Boston

Over its 130-year-plus history, Boston's Museum of Fine Arts (MFA) has collected some 450,000 pieces from an array of cultures and civilizations, ranging from ancient Egyptian tomb treasures to stylish modern artworks. In 2010, the museum opened its long-anticipated Art of The Americas wing, designed by Norman Foster, which displays works created in North, Central, and South America.

Museum façade, Huntington Avenue

○ The MFA boasts four restaurants and cafés, escalating in quality and price as you move from the courtyard level upward.

○ The MFA's Family Art Cart in the Shapiro Family Courtyard provides activities and materials to use in the galleries. Consult the museum's website for a full schedule of events.

Admission to the museum on Wednesdays 4–9:45pm is by voluntary donation.

• 465 Huntington Ave (Ave of the Arts)
• Map D6
• 617 267 9300
• www.mfa.org
• "T" station: Museum (green line/E train)
• open: 10am–4:45pm Mon & Tue, 10am–9:45pm Wed–Fri, 10am–4:45pm Sat & Sun • Adm: \$22

Top 10 Features

1. *La Japonaise*
2. Japanese Temple Room
3. John Singer Sargent Murals
4. John Singleton Copley Portraits
5. Statue of King Aspelta
6. Egyptian Royal Pectoral
7. *Postman Joseph Roulin*
8. Silverwork by Paul Revere
9. *Dance at Bougival*
10. *Christ in Majesty with Symbols*

La Japonaise
Claude Monet's 1876 portrait *(below)* reflects a time when Japanese culture fascinated Europe's most style-conscious circles. The model, interestingly, is Monet's wife, Camille.

Japanese Temple Room
With its wood paneling and subdued lighting, the Temple Room evokes ancient Japanese shrines atop mist-enshrouded mountains. The statues, which date from as early as the seventh century, depict prominent figures from Buddhist texts.

John Singer Sargent Murals
Having secured some of Sargent's most important portraiture in the early 20th century, the MFA went one step further and commissioned the artist to paint murals and bas-reliefs on its central rotunda and colonnade *(left)*.

→ For more art, visit the neighboring Isabella Stewart Gardner Museum See pp28–9

4 John Singleton Copley Portraits

The self-taught, Boston-born Copley made a name for himself by painting the most affluent and influential Bostonians of his day, from pre-Revolutionary figures like John Hancock *(left)* to early American presidents.

Fenway entrance

Huntington Ave entrance

Key to Floorplan

▬	Lower Ground floor
▬	First floor
▬	Second floor
▬	Third floor

5 Statue of King Aspelta

This statue of the great 6th-century BC Nubian king, Aspelta, was recovered in 1920 at Nuri in present-day Sudan during a MFA/Harvard joint expedition.

7 Postman Joseph Roulin

The MFA boasts some of Vincent van Gogh's most important work, including this 1888 oil, which was painted during his stay in Arles, France.

6 Egyptian Royal Pectoral

This extremely rare chest ornament *(above)* is nearly 4,000 years old. A vulture is depicted with a cobra on its left wing, ready to strike.

8 Silverwork by Paul Revere

Famed for his midnight ride, Revere *(see p38)* was also known for his masterful silverwork. The breadth of his ability is apparent in the museum's 200-piece collection, including this Sons of Liberty bowl *(below)*.

Gallery Guide

European, Classical, Far Eastern, and Egyptian art and artifacts occupy the original MFA building. The informative Visitor Center is located on Level 1. The Linde Wing for Contemporary Art, on the west side of the museum, also houses the museum shop, cafés, and a restaurant. Arts from the Americas are spread across four levels in the Art of The Americas wing, on the east side of the museum. The wing has 53 galleries, plus a state-of-the-art auditorium, and displays over 5,000 works of art.

9 Dance at Bougival

This endearing image (1883) of a couple dancing is among Renoir's most beloved works. It exemplifies the artist's knack for taking a timeless situation and modernizing it by dressing his subjects in the latest fashions.

10 Christ in Majesty with Symbols

Acquired in 1919 from a small Spanish church, this medieval fresco had an amazingly complex journey to Boston, which involved waterproofing it with lime and Parmesan for safe transport.

Left **Installation, Textile & Fashion Arts Collection** Right **Coffins, Art of Egypt Collection**

Museum of Fine Arts Collections

1 Art of Asia

For Japanese art connoisseurs, the museum offers a dizzying overview of Japan's multiple artistic forms. In fact, the MFA holds the largest collection of ancient Japanese art outside of Japan. In addition to the tranquil Temple Room *(see p22)*, with its centuries-old Buddhist statues, visitors should admire the beautiful hanging scrolls and woodblock prints, with their magical, dramatic landscapes and spirited renderings of everyday life. Kurasawa fans will be enthralled by the menacing samurai weaponry. Additionally, the Art of Asia collection boasts exquisite objects from 2,000 years of Chinese, Indian, and Southeast Asian history, including sensuous ivory figurines, pictorial carpets, and vibrant watercolors.

2 Art of Egypt, Nubia, & the Ancient Near East

This collection is a treasure trove of millennia-old Egyptian sarcophagi, tomb finds, and Nubian

Marble busts, Classical Art Collection

jewelry and objects from everyday life. The assemblage of Egyptian funerary pieces, including beautifully crafted jewelry and intact ceramic urns is awe-inspiring. Ancient Near Eastern artifacts, with their bold iconography and rich materials, illustrate why the region was known as the Cradle of Civilization.

3 Classical Art

The remarkable Classical Art Collection has a hoard of gold bracelets, glass, mosaic bowls, and stately marble busts. One of the earliest pieces is a c.1500 BC gold axe, inscribed with symbols from a still-undeciphered Cretan language.

4 Art of The Americas

The MFA's Art of The Americas wing, designed by Norman Foster, opened in 2010. The wing features pieces dating from pre-Columbian times, through to the third quarter of the 20th century, and showcases about 5,000 works produced in North, Central, and South America. The museum has profited from generous benefactors over the years and the collection boasts the world's finest collection of colonial New England furniture, rare 17th-century American portraiture, a superb display of American silver, and paintings by the country's own "Old" Masters, including Copley, Stuart, Cole, Sargent, Cassat, Homer, and many others.

5 European Art to 1900

From 12th-century tempera baptism scenes to Claude Monet's *Haystacks*, the MFA's European collection is staggeringly diverse. Painstakingly transferred medieval stained-glass windows, beautifully illuminated bibles, and delicate French tapestries are displayed alongside works by Old Masters. Titian, El Greco, Rembrandt, and Rubens. The superlative Impressionist collection boasts the likes of Monet, Renoir, Degas, and Cézanne.

Grand piano, Musical Instruments Collection

6 Textile & Fashion Arts

Rotating displays highlight pictorial quilts, period fashions, fine Persian rugs, and pre-colonial Andean weavings. Particularly interesting are the museum's holdings of textiles and costumes from the Elizabethan and Stuart periods – an unprecedented 1943 donation from the private collection of Elizabeth Day McCormick.

African mask, Art of Africa Collection

7 Contemporary Art

Given Boston's affinity for the traditional, you might be surprised by this world-class collection of contemporary and late 20th-century art. It includes the work of the painter and photographer Chuck Close and the abstract Expressionist artist Jackson Pollock, both of which are on display in the Art of The Americas wing.

8 Musical Instruments

Priceless 17th-century guitars, ornately inlaid pianos, and even a mouth organ are on view to visitors of the MFA. Among the more distinctive pieces is the c.1796 English grand piano – the earliest extant example of a piano with a six-octave range – and a 1680 French guitar by the Voboam workshop.

9 Art of Africa and Oceania

Pre-colonial artifacts from these collections include Melanese canoe ornaments, dramatic Congolese bird sculptures and African funerary art. The most popular African display is the powerful looking 19th- and 20th-century wooden masks.

10 "Please be Seated!" Installations

View one of the country's most comprehensive collections of American contemporary furniture at the MFA. The museum encourages visitors to admire and sit on these furniture pieces. Take a break and have a seat on fine American handiwork by designers such as Maloof, Castle, and Eames.

Trinity Church

Boston has a knack for creating curious visual juxtapositions, and one of the most remarkable is in Copley Square, where H. H. Richardson's 19th-century Romanesque Trinity Church reflects in the blue-tinted glass of the decidedly 20th-century John Hancock Tower. The breathtakingly beautiful church was named a National Historic Landmark in 1971 and has earned the American Institute of Architects' distinction of being among the ten greatest buildings in the country.

Trinity Church façade

🍴 Grab a quick bite at the Prudential Center food court, just two blocks away (800 Boylston St).

🕑 From September to June organ recitals are held every Friday, 12:15–12:45pm. By donation.

Please remember that Trinity Church is a place of worship.

Tours of the church are available and begin in the Shop at Trinity on the Boylston Street side of the complex.

• 206 Clarendon St
• Map L5
• "T" station: Copley Sq (green line) & Back Bay (orange line)
• 617 536 0944 (church)
• www.trinitychurch boston.org
• Church open for self-tours 9am–5pm Mon, Fri & Sat, 9am–6pm Tue–Thu, 1–6pm Sun
• Shop open 9am–5pm Mon, Fri & Sat, 9am–6pm Tue–Thu & Sun
• Adm: $7; tours: $7

Top 10 Features

1 La Farge Windows
2 Burne-Jones Windows
3 Central Tower
4 Front Façade & Side Towers
5 Organ Pipes
6 Phillips Brooks' Bust
7 Pulpit Carving
8 Embroidered Kneelers
9 The Shop at Trinity
10 The Foundation

Burne-Jones Windows

Edward Burne-Jones' windows – on the Boylston Street side – were inspired by the burgeoning English Arts & Crafts Movement. Its influence is readily apparent in his *David's Charge to Solomon (below)*, with its bold patterning and colors.

Central Tower

The church's central tower borrows its square design from the Cathedral of Salamanca, Spain. On the interior, wall paintings by La Farge depicting biblical figures in vibrant hues are in sharp contrast to the austere church interiors of the artist's day.

La Farge Windows

A newcomer to stained glasswork at the time, John La Farge approached his commissions (like *Christ in Majesty, below*) with the same sense of daring and vitality that Richardson employed in his Trinity design.

Front Façade & Side Towers

Inspired by the Romanesque church of St Trophime in Arles, France, Richardson redesigned Trinity's front portico as well as two new side towers. The additions were implemented by his firm of architects some years after his death in the 1890s.

For more on attractions in Back Bay See pp80–83

Organ Pipes

The beautiful organ pipes frame the church's west wall *(left)*. Exquisitely designed, ornately painted, and – of course – very sonorous, the pipes seem to hug the church's ceiling arches.

Phillips Brooks' Bust
Keeping watch over the baptismal font is Rector Brooks. Renowned for his sermons – bold, forthright, and fresh for their time – he was rector at Trinity from 1869–91.

Pulpit Carving
Preachers throughout the ages, including St Paul, Martin Luther, and Phillips Brooks of Trinity *(right)*, are depicted in high relief on the pulpit designed by Charles Coolidge.

Church Floorplan

Embroidered Kneelers
Trinity's colorful kneelers have been stitched by parishioners in memory of people and events past. They serve as an informal folk history of the congregation.

The Shop at Trinity
Apart from a wide range of religious books and other items, the store also sells exclusive works by local artists and CDs of the Trinity Choir.

Trinity Sings "Hallelujah"

One of Boston's most cherished traditions is the singing of Handel's *Messiah* and its unmistakable "Hallelujah Chorus" at Trinity during the Christmas season. Hundreds pack the sanctuary to experience the choir's ethereal, masterful treatment of the piece. Call 617 536 0944 for performance information.

The Foundation
As part of 34-year-old Richardson's daring plan, the first of 4,500 wooden support pilings for the church was driven into the spongy Back Bay landfill in 1873. Rev. Phillips Brooks laid the cornerstone two years later.

For more H. H. Richardson buildings **See p19**

Isabella Stewart Gardner Museum

One needn't be a patron of the arts to be wowed by the Gardner Museum. Its namesake traveled tirelessly to acquire a world-class art collection, which is housed in a Venetian-style palazzo where flowers bloom, sculpted nudes pose in hidden corners, and entire ceilings reveal their European origins. The palace is complemented by a striking modern building, designed by Renzo Piano, which holds an intimate performance hall, galleries, and a charming café.

Isabella Stewart Gardner

🍴 Light salads and sandwiches are served in the museum's café. Weather permitting, request a table outdoors in the garden.

🎵 The museum's Calderwood Hall hosts a concert series in the spring and fall. See museum website for more information.

Gardner After Hours, on the third Thursday of each month, hosts live jazz, a wine bar, and games late into the evening

• "T" station: Museum (green line/E train)
• 280 The Fenway
• Map D6
• 617 566 1401
• www.gardner museum.org
• open 11am–5pm Wed–Mon (to 9pm Thu)
• Adm: $15; free to anyone named Isabella.

Top 10 Features

1. The Courtyard
2. Dutch Room
3. Gothic Room
4. Titian Room
5. Long Gallery
6. Raphael Room
7. Tapestry Room
8. Macknight, Yellow, & Blue Rooms
9. Spanish Cloister
10. Veronese Room

Dutch Room
The space that houses some of Gardner's most impressive acquisitions *(below)* was the scene of an incredible art heist in 1990: among the 13 works stolen were a Vermeer and two Rembrandts.

Gothic Room
Appreciate John Singer Sargent's splendid and somewhat risqué 1888 portrait of Mrs Gardner as well as medieval liturgical artwork from the 13th century.

The Courtyard
Gardner integrated Roman, Byzantine, Romanesque, Renaissance, and Gothic elements in the magnificent courtyard *(below)*, which is out of bounds but can be viewed through the graceful arches surrounding it.

Titian Room
The most artistically significant gallery was conceived by Gardner as the palazzo's grand reception hall. It has a distinctly Italian flavor and showcases Titian's *Europa (left)*, one of the greatest masterpieces in the US.

For more art, visit the neighboring Museum of Fine Arts
See pp22–5

Long Gallery

5 Roman sculptural fragments and busts line glass cases crammed with unusual 15th- and 16th-century books and artifacts. One such rare tome is a 1481 copy of Dante's *The Divine Comedy*, featuring drawings by Botticelli.

Raphael Room

6 Gardner was the first collector to bring works by Raphael to the US; three of the artist's major works are on display here *(left)*, alongside Botticelli's *Tragedy of Lucretia* and Crivelli's *St. George and the Dragon*.

Macknight, Yellow, & Blue Rooms

8 Fans of the Impressionists need look no further than these rooms *(above)*, which house portraits and sketches by the likes of Manet, Matisse, Degas, and Sargent. Of particular note is Sargent's *Mrs. Gardner in White*.

Spanish Cloister

9 With stunning mosaic tiling and a Moorish arch, the Spanish Cloister looks like a hidden patio at the Alhambra. But Sargent's sweeping *El Jaleo* (1882, *below*), all sultry shadows and rich hues, gives the room its distinctiveness.

Veronese Room

10 With its richly gilded and painted Spanish-leather wallcoverings, it's easy to miss this gallery's highlight: look up at Paolo Veronese's 16th-century masterwork *The Coronation of Hebe*.

Key to Floorplan

  First floor

  Second floor

  Third floor

Tapestry Room

7 Restored to its original 1914 state, this sweeping gallery houses two 16th-century Belgian tapestry cycles: one depicting *Scenes from the Life of Cyrus the Great* and the other *Scenes from the Life of Abraham*.

Fenway Court

Before Isabella Stewart Gardner died in 1924 she stipulated in her will that Fenway Court (as it was then known) and her collection become a public museum. She believed that works of art should be displayed in a setting that would fire the imagination. So the collection, exhibited over three floors, is not arranged chronologically or by country of origin but organized purely to enhance the viewing of the individual treasures. To encourage visitors to respond to the artworks themselves, many of the 2,500 objects – from ancient Egyptian pieces to Matisse's paintings – are left unlabeled, as Gardner had requested.

Charlestown Navy Yard

Some of the most storied battleships in American naval history began life at Charlestown Navy Yard. Established in 1800 as one of the country's first naval yards, Charlestown remained vital to US security until its decommissioning in 1974. From the 200-year-old wooden-hulled <u>USS Constitution</u> to the <u>World War II-era steel destroyer USS Cassin Young</u>, the yard gives visitors an all-hands-on-deck historical experience unparalleled in America.

1 USS Constitution

First tested in action during the War of 1812, the USS *Constitution* (below) is the world's oldest warship still afloat. A tugboat helps her perform an annual turnaround cruise on July 4th.

Defensive guns

🍺 Try some pub grub at the atmospheric 18th-century Warren Tavern (2 Pleasant St).

🔎 Visitors must pass through a metal detector to board the USS *Constitution*.

• Visitors' Center: Building Number 5 • Map H2 • 617 242 5601 • www. nps.gov/bost • "T": North Station (green & orange lines) • Water shuttle from Long Wharf, www. mbta.com • Bunker Hill Monument: open 9am–5pm daily; last climb 4:30pm • Naval Yard Visitors' Center: open 9am–5pm daily • USS Cassin Young: open 10am–4pm daily • USS Constitution: 10am–4pm Tue–Sun (Thu–Sun in winter) • USS Constitution Museum: open 10am–5pm daily (9am–6pm summer). Donation. • Many sites remain open one hour later in summer

Top 10 Sights

1. USS *Constitution*
2. Bunker Hill Monument
3. Navy Yard Visitors' Center
4. Marine Railway
5. USS *Constitution* Museum
6. Ropewalk
7. Dry Dock #1
8. Commandant's House
9. Muster House
10. USS *Cassin Young*

2 Bunker Hill Monument

Ten minutes' walk from the yard is this 220-ft (67-m) granite obelisk *(below)*, which has towered over Charlestown since 1842. It commemorates the first major battle of the American Revolution *(see p10)*.

3 Navy Yard Visitors' Center

Begin your stroll through the Yard at the National Park Service-operated Visitors' Center, where you can pick up literature about the site's many attractions and check on tour schedules.

4 Marine Railway

The Navy Yard constantly evolved to meet changing demands and developments. The marine railway was built in 1918 to haul submarines and other vessels out of the water for hull repairs.

 Note: Admission to all sights at Charlestown Navy Yard is free or by donation

5 USS *Constitution* Museum

With enough activities to keep kids entertained and plenty of nautical trivia to satisfy a naval historian, this museum brings USS *Constitution's* 200 years to life. This watercolor *(left)* on ivory is of 19th-century naval hero Commodore William Bainbridge.

Charlestown Navy Yard

6 Ropewalk

This quarter-mile-long (0.5 km) building (1837) houses steam-powered machinery that produced rope rigging for the nation's warships.

7 Dry Dock #1

To facilitate hull repairs on the navy's ships, Dry Dock #1 *(right)* was opened in 1833. The granite dock was drained by massive steam-powered pumps. USS *Constitution* was the first ship to be given an overhaul here.

8 Commandant's House

The oldest building in the yard (1805) housed the commandants of the First Naval District. With its sweeping harbor views and wraparound porch, this elegant mansion *(left)* was ideal for entertaining dignitaries from all over the world.

9 Muster House

This octagonal brick building was designed in the Georgian-revival style popular in the northeast in the mid-19th-century. The house served as an administration hub, where the Yard's clerical work was carried out.

10 USS *Cassin Young*

Never defeated, despite withstanding multiple kamikaze bomber-attacks in the Pacific, this World War II era destroyer *(left)* could be considered USS *Constitution's* 20th-century successor.

Old Ironsides

Given her 25-inch (63-cm) thick hull at the waterline, it's easy to imagine why USS *Constitution* earned her nickname "Old Ironsides." Pitted against HMS *Guerriere* during the War of 1812, the ship engaged its enemy in a shoot-out that left *Guerriere* all but destroyed. Upon witnessing British cannon balls "bouncing" off USS *Constitution's* hull, a sailor allegedly exclaimed, "Huzzah! Her sides are made of iron." The rest is history.

Note: Muster House, Commandant's House, and the Ropewalk are closed to the public

10 New England Aquarium

The sea pervades nearly every aspect of Boston life, so it's appropriate that the New England Aquarium is one of the city's most popular attractions. What sets this aquarium apart from similar institutions is its commitment to presenting not only an exciting environment to learn about marine life, but also to conserving the natural habitats of its gilled, feathered, and whiskered inhabitants.

Aquarium façade

If the aquarium has not convinced you to eliminate fish from your diet, visit Legal Harborside for a leisurely, moderately priced meal *(see p42)*. Quick, quality bites from around the globe can also be had at the Quincy Market food hall, three blocks away.

Purchase discount combination tickets for the aquarium along with an IMAX film or a whale-watching excursion.

• "T" station: Aquarium (blue line) • Central Wharf • Map R3 • 617 973 5200 • www.neaq.org for general info, including current IMAX features • Open 9am–5pm Mon–Fri, 9am–6pm Sat & Sun (extended hours Jul–Aug) • Adm: $22.95 • Whale Watch: 617 973 5206 for reservations and rate information • IMAX: call 866 815 IMAX (4629) for show times; Adm: $9.95

Top 10 Features

1. Penguin Pool
2. Tropical Gallery
3. Giant Ocean Tank
4. IMAX Theater
5. Harbor Seal Tanks
6. Marine Mammal Center
7. Whale Watch
8. Amazing Jellies
9. Shark and Ray Touch Tank
10. Edge of the Sea

Tropical Gallery

A Pacific coral reef *(right)* bustles with unicorn tangs, bird wrasses, and blue-striped cleaner fish, to name but a few of the vibrant inhabitants of these exhibits, which are made of painted artificial coral.

Giant Ocean Tank

Offering a veritable cross-section of a Caribbean reef, the Giant Ocean Tank packs sea turtles, sharks, moray eels, brightly colored tropical fish *(above)*, and scores of other species into the 200,000-gallon (900,000-liter) tank.

Penguin Pool

Four species of penguins – northern and southern Rockhoppers *(above)*, Little Blue, and African – compete for space on the central island and take dips in the pool.

IMAX Theater

The Simons IMAX Theater shows large-format 3D documentaries, featuring digital surround sound and plenty of breathtaking, you-are-there cinematic moments. Education with an adrenalin rush.

Harbor Seal Tanks

Harbor seals swim, feed, and play in specially designed tanks outside the aquarium. All have either been born in captivity or rescued and deemed unfit for release into the wild.

For more information on Whale Watch excursions **See p137**

Marine Mammal Center

Observe Northern fur seals as they frolic in an open-air exhibit at the edge of the Boston harbor. Meet the seals and sea lions face-to-face at the large observation deck.

Whale Watch

The aquarium's extremely popular whale watch ships (Apr–Oct only) provide an unparalleled glimpse into the life cycles of the world's largest mammals *(left)*. *Voyager III* steams well outside Boston Harbor to the Stellwagen Bank, a prime feeding area for pods of whales.

Entrance

Key to Floorplan

■	Ground Floor
■	Mezzanine
■	First Floor

Amazing Jellies

The 5,000-sq-ft (465-sq-m) exhibit includes thousands of jellies from a huge variety of species. You'll learn why jelly populations are increasing all around the world and the part played by humans.

Shark and Ray Touch Tank

The largest of its kind on the US east coast, this 25,000-gallon (95,000-liter) mangrove-themed tank is surrounded by shallow edges and viewing windows, allowing visitors to roll up their sleeves to feel the almost velvety wings of stingrays and the abrasive skin of sharks.

Edge of the Sea

For those not content to merely gaze at fish behind glass, the Edge of the Sea tidepool exhibit puts marine life at visitors' fingertips – literally *(below)*. Inside a ground-level fiberglass tank, the New England seashore is recreated in all its diversity.

The Aquarium's Mission

The aquarium's aim, first and foremost, is to instigate and support marine conservation. Its Conservation Action Fund has fought on behalf of endangered marine animals worldwide, helping to protect humpback whales in the South Pacific, sea turtles in New England, and dolphins in Peru.

Following pages **Swan Boats, Boston Common**

Battle of Concord Bridge

🔟 Moments in Boston History

1 1630: Boston Founded
Under the leadership of John Winthrop *(see p38)*, English Puritans moved from overcrowded Charlestown and colonized the Shawmut Peninsula. Permission was granted from its sole English inhabitant, Anglican cleric William Blaxton. Their city on the hill was named Boston in honor of the native English town of their leaders.

2 1636: Harvard Created
Boston's Puritan leaders established a college at Newtowne (later Cambridge) to educate future generations of clergy. When young Charlestown minister John Harvard died two years later and left his books and half his money to the college, it was renamed Harvard *(see p16)*.

3 1775: American Revolution
Friction between colonists and the British crown had been building for more than a decade when British troops marched on

Gates, Harvard University

Detail, Boston Library

Lexington to confiscate rebel weapons. Forewarned by Paul Revere *(see p38)*, local militia, known as the Minute Men, skirmished with British regulars on Lexington Green. During the second confrontation at Concord, the shot heard round the world marked the beginning of the Revolution, which ended in American independence with the 1783 Treaty of Paris.

4 1845: Irish Arrived
Irish fleeing the potato famine arrived in Boston in tens of thousands, many eventually settling in the south of the city. By 1900, the Irish were the dominant ethnic group in Boston. They flexed their political muscle accordingly, culminating in the election of John F. Kennedy *(see p39)* as president in 1960.

5 1848: Boston Public Library Founded
The Boston Public Library was established as the first publicly supported municipal library in the US. In 1895 the library moved into the Italianate "palace of the people" on Copley Square *(see p81)*.

6 1863: Black Boston Went to War
Following decades of agitation to abolish slavery, the city sent the country's first African-American

For more on Boston's revolutionary history **See p10**

regiment to join Union forces in the Civil War. The regiment was honored by the Shaw Memorial on Boston Common *(see p14).*

1897: Subway Opened
The Tremont Street subway, the first underground in the US, was opened on September 1 to ease road congestion. It cost $4.4 million to construct and the initial fare was five cents. The Metropolitan Boston Transit Authority (MBTA) now transports 1.2 million people daily.

1958: Freedom Trail Opened
This historical walking tour connects the city's sights. It was based on a 1951 *Boston Herald Traveler* column by William Scofield, and was the first of its kind in the US.

The Big Dig

2004: Sox Win
The Boston Red Sox overcame an alleged 86 year-old sporting curse to win baseball's World Series for the first time since 1918. The team thrilled fans of "Red Sox Nation" by winning again in 2007.

2008: The Big Dig
The $15 billion highway project to alleviate traffic congestion is largely completed. As a result, the city has gained new park space and the soaring Zakim Bridge, the world's widest cable-stayed bridge.

Top 10 Innovations

1 Sewing Machine
Elias Howe invented the sewing machine in Cambridge in 1845, but spent decades securing patent rights.

2 Surgical Anesthesia
Ether was first used for anesthesia at Massachusetts General Hospital in 1846.

3 Telephone
Alexander Graham Bell invented the telephone in his Boston laboratory in 1876.

4 Safety Razor
Bostonian King Camp Gillette invented the safety razor with disposable blades in 1901.

5 Mutual Fund
Massachusetts Investors Trust opened in 1924 as the first modern mutual fund that pooled investor's money to purchase portfolio stocks.

6 Programmable Digital Computer
A Harvard team built the first programmable digital computer, Mark 1, in 1946. Its 750,000 components weighed about 10,000 lb (454 kg).

7 Microwave Oven
A Raytheon company engineer placed popcorn in front of a radar tube in 1946 and discovered the principle behind the microwave oven.

8 Instant Film
Cambridge inventor Edwin Land devised the Polaroid camera, launched in 1948.

9 E-mail
Ray Tomlinson, an engineer at Bolt, Beranek, and Newman in Cambridge, sent the first e-mail message in 1971.

10 Facebook
Harvard student Mark Zuckerberg posted the first message to Facemash (Facebook's predecessor) in 2003.

Note: The MIT Museum highlights many Boston and Cambridge technological breakthroughs **See p121**

Left **John F. Kennedy** Right **James Michael Curley** (seated)

Figures in Boston History

1 John Winthrop (1587–1649)

Acting on a daring plan put together by English Puritans in 1629, Winthrop led approximately 800 settlers to the New World to build a godly civilization in the wilderness. He settled his Puritan charges at Boston in 1630 (see p36) and served as the governor of the new Massachusetts Bay Colony until his death.

2 Increase Mather (1639–1723)

Educated at Harvard, preacher Increase Mather solidified the hold of Puritan theologians on the Massachusetts government. When William took the English crown, Mather persuaded the king to grant a charter that gave the colony the right to elect the council of the governor in 1691. His influence was later undermined by his support of the 1692 Salem witch trials.

Mary Baker Eddy

3 Samuel Adams (1722–1803)

Failed businessman Samuel Adams became Boston's master politician in the tumultuous years leading up to the revolution (see p10). Adams signed the Declaration of Independence and served in both Continental Congresses. As governor of Massachusetts, he joined Paul Revere in laying the cornerstone of the State House (see p11) in 1795.

4 Paul Revere (1735–1818)

Best known for his "midnight ride" to forewarn the rebels of the British march on Concord, Revere served the American Revolution as organizer, messenger, and propagandist. A gifted silversmith with many pieces in the Museum of Fine Arts (see p22–5), he founded the metal-working firm that gilded the State House dome and sheathed the hull of the USS Constitution.

5 Harrison Gray Otis (1765–1848)

In the 1790s, Harrison Gray Otis and James Mason transformed Beacon Hill from a hilly pasture into a chic neighborhood that embodies the Federal building style. Otis championed the architecture of Charles Bulfinch, and three of his Bulfinch-designed houses still grace Beacon Hill, including the one now known as Harrison Gray Otis House (see p76).

6 Donald McKay (1810–1880)

McKay built the largest and swiftest of the clipper ships in his East Boston shipyard in 1850. The speedy vessels revolutionized long-distance shipping at the time of the California gold rush and gave Boston its last glory days as a mercantile port before the rise of rail transport.

Mary Baker Eddy (1821–1910)

After recovering from a major accident, Eddy wrote *Science and Health with Key to the Scriptures*, the basis of Christian Science. She founded a church in Boston in 1879, and in 1892 reorganized it as the First Church of Christ, Scientist *(see p82)*. Eddy also established the Pulitzer prize-winning *Christian Science Monitor* newspaper in 1908.

James Michael Curley (1874–1958)

Self-proclaimed champion of "the little people," Curley used patronage and Irish pride to retain a stranglehold on Boston politics from his election as mayor in 1914 until his defeat at the polls in 1949. Known as "the rascal king" he embodied political corruption but created many enduring public works.

John F. Kennedy (1917–1963)

Grandson of Irish American mayor John "Honey Fitz" Fitzgerald and son of ambassador Joseph Kennedy, John F. Kennedy represented Boston in both houses of the US Congress before he became the first Roman Catholic elected president of the United States. The presidential library at Columbia Point exhibits his brief, but intense, period in office *(see p129)*.

W. Arthur Garrity, Jr. (1920–1999)

In 1974, US District Court judge Garrity ruled that African-American students had been denied their constitutional rights to the best available education. He ordered a desegregation plan for Boston's 200 schools, setting off protests, some violent, in predominantly white neighborhoods.

Literary Bostonians

Anne Bradstreet
Bradstreet (c.1612–72) was America's first poet, publishing *The Tenth Muse, Lately Sprung Up in America* in 1650.

Ralph Waldo Emerson
Poet and philosopher, Emerson (1803–82) espoused transcendentalism and pioneered American literary independence.

Henry Wadsworth Longfellow
Known for epic poems such as *Hiawatha*, Longfellow (1807–82) also translated Dante.

Louisa May Alcott
Little Women sealed Alcott's (1832–88) literary fame, but she also acted as a nurse in the Civil War.

Henry James
Master of sonorous prose, James (1843–1916) is considered one of the creators of the psychological novel.

Dorothy West
African-American novelist and essayist West (1907–98) made sharp observations about class and race conflicts.

Robert Lowell
Lowell's (1917–77) "confessional poetry" influenced a generation of writers.

Robert Parker
Scholar of mystery literature, Parker (1932–2010) is best known for his signature detective Spenser.

Robert Pinsky
Poet, critic, and translator, Pinsky (b.1940) served as US poet laureate and now teaches at Boston University.

Dennis Lehane
Novelist Dennis Lehane (b.1965) brings a dark, tragic vision to the working-class neighborhoods of Boston.

Note: Portraits of many famous Bostonians painted 1760–1820 are displayed at the Museum of Fine Arts **See p22–5**

Left **Upstairs on the Square** Right **L'Espalier**

🔟 Restaurants

1 Harvest

For 40 years, this relaxed restaurant has been a leader in setting the direction of American cuisine. Chef Mary Dumont re-interprets New England classics, matching monkfish with artichokes and cockles, or filling ricotta gnocchi with butternut squash and sautéeing them in pumpkin seed oil. ◉ 44 Brattle St, Cambridge • Map B1 • 617 868 2255 • $$$$$

2 Rialto

Chef Jody Adams takes a luscious and delicately innovative approach to Mediterranean cuisine, working magic with a simple basil cream soup, or using grilled tomatoes to give extra depth to her gazpacho. A green olive and balsamic vinegar sauce perfectly balances the unctuousness of her signature roasted marinated duck. The comfortable and soothing dining room is ideal for special occasions. Dinner only. ◉ Charles Hotel, 1 Bennett St, Cambridge • Map B2 • 617 661 5050 • $$$$$

3 Hamersley's Bistro

Chef-owner Gordon Hamersley presides over this defining South End restaurant. The menu is inspired by French provincial cooking but features the best of mostly local produce (don't miss the lemon-infused broiled chicken). The bar scene is lively, and the outdoor dining tables provide one of the neighborhood's prime social settings in summer (see p111).

4 Clio

One of the country's most lauded young chefs, award-winning Ken Oringer is dedicated to innovation and experimentation. With an ever-changing menu he always looks for new flavor sensations. For instance, few Boston chefs would dare to serve bone marrow custard with nougats of wild mushrooms and black truffles. Reservations are recommended (see p89).

5 Trade

Trade is the fine-dining anchor to the Greenway Park that links downtown and the waterfront. Set in the environmentally friendly Atlantic Wharf building, it makes use of great Mediterranean flavors while remaining true to its New England roots. Both ends of that historic trade route shine in braised short rib with sunchokes, orange, and olives. ◉ 540 Atlantic Ave • Map H4 • 617 451 1234 • $$$

6 L'Espalier

Adjoining the luxury Mandarin Oriental Hotel (see p146), this is one of Boston's top restaurants. The award-winning, modern French cuisine emphasizes local, artisanal ingredients, producing dishes such as butter-poached Maine lobster and cocoa-rubbed venison. Only expensive fixed-price and tasting menus are offered during dinner service. A top-class venue in the heart of fashionable Back Bay (see p89).

Note: For more restaurants and key to price categories **See pp89, 95, 103, 111, 117, 125, 131**

Menton
Superchef Barbara Lynch's glamorous Fort Point dining room serves hearty, sophisticated food to match. Lardo-wrapped tuna with golden raisins and pine nuts evokes Sicily, while roasted duck with redcurrants is quintessentially French. Four-course and seven-course dinners only. ◈ *354 Congress St • Map H5 • 617 737 0099 • $$$$$*

Upstairs on the Square
Gloriously over-the-top decor complements the New American and Italian cuisine at this Harvard Square favorite. A soirée dining room serves the likes of roasted halibut with lavender-lemon potatoes at exquisitely laid tables, while more casual, less pricey dishes are available downstairs in the Monday Club Bar. ◈ *19 Winthrop St, Cambridge • Map B1 • 617 864 1933 • $$$$*

Meritage
Chef Daniel Bruce of the Boston Harbor Hotel pairs his creative small plates with six different wine styles. Seared yellowfin tuna rolled in black pepper, for example, fits a spicy red, while roasted grey sole

Radius

topped with caviar calls for a refreshing sparkling white wine. ◈ *70 Rowes Wharf • Map H4 • 617 439 3995 • $$$$$*

Radius
Chef Michael Schlow is a stickler for detail and blends multiple flavors for a single, clear taste fusion in his own version of New American cuisine. You'd think seared Maine scallops might get lost when combined with wild mushrooms, potato puree, leeks, and a truffle emulsion, but the woodsy flavors just enhance the sweet, salty taste of the sea. The restaurant is regularly mobbed by successful CEOs and their more glamorous stockholders *(see p103)*.

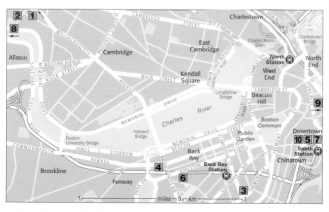

Note: Even restaurants that are booked weeks ahead will often have seats available for diners willing to eat at 6pm or earlier

Left **Barking Crab** Right **East Coast Grill**

🔟 Spots for Seafood

Barking Crab
This colorful fish shack is most congenial in the summer, when diners sit outdoors at picnic tables. Most of the local fish – cod, haddock, tuna, halibut, clams, and crab – are so fresh that they need only the most basic preparation. ◈ *88 Sleeper St • Map H4 • 617 426 2722 • $$*

Legal Harborside
The flagship of the Legal Sea Foods chain makes dockside dining chic, with a no-frills, casual dining room and oyster bar on level one; fine dining and beautifully fresh fish on level two; and cocktails, fish tacos, and snacks on level three. All three experiences come with a stunning harbor view. ◈ *Long Wharf & other locations • Map H3 • 617 742 5300 • $$*

East Coast Grill
This restaurant pioneered the concept of casual fine dining, capitalizing on the skill of the staff in cooking seafood over the smoke and heat of an open fire. Hot spices abound, with chefs perking up a bland fish with a peppery basting sauce or toning down an oily fish with a citrus marinade. The simple, unfussy dining room ensures that the food is the focus of attention. Reservations are not accepted so arrive early and be prepared to wait – it's worth it. ◈ *1271 Cambridge St, Cambridge • Map E2 • 617 491 6568 • Closed lunch Mon–Sat • $$*

Mare Oyster Bar
Fine dining and health-conscious eating converge in Mare's Italian coastal cuisine. Begin with the shellfish raw bar, then savour some of the classic seafood pasta dishes, grilled fish, and delicious crudos – or treat yourself with Mare's decadent lobster roll on brioche. A few meat dishes are also available. ◈ *135 Richmond St • 617 723 4273 • Closed lunch Mon • $$$$*

No Name Restaurant
As Fish Pier's only restaurant, No Name has an intimate relationship with the fishermen who both sell their catch to, and eat at, this bare-bones restaurant. The equally very basic menu consists mostly of fried fish. The great chowder is what fishermen call "trim" chowder – full of hunks of whatever has been boned and trimmed that day. ◈ *15½ Fish Pier • 617 423 2705 • $*

O Ya
Combining Japanese tradition and American invention, this elegant 37-seat restaurant proves that good things come in small packages. Half the menu is sushi and sashimi, the other half meat and vegetarian. With six chefs at work, each bite-sized portion is exquisitely executed. Ask for the *omakase* (tasting) menu and let head chef Tim Cushman wow you with a culinary tour de force. ◈ *9 East St • Map H5 • 617 654 9900 • Closed lunch Sun, Mon • $$$$$*

For more restaurants and key to price categories **See pp89, 95, 103, 111, 117, 125, 131**

James Hook & Co.

A family-owned business located right on Fort Point Channel, Hooks is primarily a broker that supplies lobster to restaurants throughout the US. However, they also cook lobster, clams, crab, and some fin fish on the spot. Take your order, sit on the sea wall, and chow down. ⏚ 15 Northern Ave • Map H5 • 617 423 5500 • Closed evenings • $

B&G Oysters

The brainchild of star chef Barbara Lynch, this brightly lit underground seafood spot is half oyster bar – there are a dozen varieties ready to be shucked at any moment – and half seafood bistro. Lynch's delicious dishes include the lobster BLT sandwich, roasted salmon with spicy Spanish chorizo, and tuna carpaccio with boiled quail egg and pickled shallot. ⏚ 550 Tremont St • 617 423 0550 • $$$$

Summer Shack

Boston celebrity chef Jasper White literally wrote the book on lobster, but he's just as adept with wood-grilled fresh fish and

Summer Shack

delicate fried shellfish. Fabulous raw bar and colorful summer fish-shack atmosphere match well with the extensive beer list. Excellent place to bring children who like to crack their own crabs. ⏚ 50 Dalton St • 617 867 9955 • Closed lunch Mon–Fri Nov–Mar • $$$

Island Creek Oyster Bar

Partly owned by the Duxbury oyster farm of the same name, this upscale, yet casual restaurant excels at shellfish (including eight varieties of New England oyster) and does great things with fin fish, too. Their seafood casserole brings together shrimp, lobster, clams, scallops, and cod in a single delectable bowl. ⏚ 500 Commonwealth Ave • Map D5 • 617 532 5300 • Closed lunch Mon–Sat • $$$

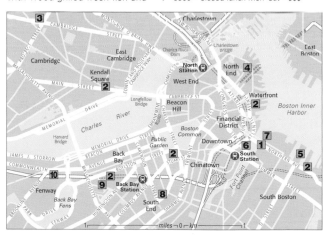

Note: At 6:30am on weekdays, the catch from Boston-based boats is auctioned in 1,000-lb (453-kilo) lots from Fish Pier

Left **Trident Booksellers & Café** Center **Frothy cappuccino** Right **Sonsie**

TOP 10 Cafés

L'Aroma Café
The beautiful people take their espresso at L'Aroma, where the Italian style of the coffees, sandwiches, luncheon salads, and pastries are more evocative of Milan than Rome. As a bonus, tea-lovers can order from a choice of 20 loose-leaf varieties *(see p87)*.

Caffè Vittoria
The jukebox at the largest of North End's Italian cafés has nearly every song ever recorded by Frank Sinatra, Tony Bennett, and Al Martino. The menu is long on short coffees and short drinks, including at least seven varieties of grappa, as well as a fair selection of Italian ices. *296 Hanover St • Map Q1*

Diesel Café
Diesel is the quintessential Davis Square gathering spot where the tragically hip rub shoulders with lesbian couples and scruffy Tufts students. The spacious café has old-fashioned booths, couches, and a pair of

1369 Coffee House

pool tables out back. The coffee menu includes a powerful double-caffeine "High Octane" brew plus teas and tisanes. *257 Elm St, Somerville*

Trident Booksellers & Café
Bibliophiles make pilgrimages to this fine bookstore. The in-store café and bar serves light and casual meals ranging from breakfast eggs to lunch wraps, as well as excellent dinner dishes like lasagna *(see p85)*.

Sonsie
Although continental breakfast is served, the scene doesn't really kick into bustling life until lunch time. By dusk, Sonsie is full of folks who just stopped in for a post-work drink and ended up making an evening of it. The food – pizza, pasta, and fusion-tinged entrées – deserves more attention than most café-goers give it *(see p87)*.

Barrington Coffee Roasting Company Café
The western Massachusetts coffee roaster Barrington Coffee brought its acclaimed selection of single-origin coffees to this artistic neighborhood at Fort Point Channel. Espresso drinks and drip coffee get equal billing, as many of the lighter roasts are best brewed one drip cup at a time. Regular tasting events are a popular feature. *346 Congress St, Fort Point • Map H5*

Recommend your favorite café on traveldk.com

1369 Coffee House

The 1369 Coffee House is as community-based as Starbucks is corporate. There is a definite neighborly atmosphere about the place. The original Inman Square branch has a more interesting cross section of ages and ethnicities but Central Square has sidewalk seating. Both branches serve mostly caffeine drinks and sweets – with sandwiches at lunch (see p123).

Thinking Cup

A cozy place to socialize on Boston Common, Thinking Cup serves teas and Stumptown Coffee. Knowledgeable baristas offer assistance with your choice of espresso drinks or pour-overs. The menu also includes tempting pastries and tasty sandwiches.
§ 165 Tremont St • Map G4

Dado Tea

However you like your tea – white, black, or green – this shop has a choice of blends to steep as a spiritually uplifting break in itself or as accompaniment to light and healthy sandwiches, wraps, and salads. Coffee-lovers are also accommodated, but tea rules here. § 955 Massachusetts Ave, Cambridge • Map C2 • 50 Church St, Cambridge • Map D1

Parish Café

During warm weather, the tables outside Parish Café offer a terrific view of the lower Back Bay street scene. Parish has some of the most creative and delicious sandwiches in the city – designed by chefs of Boston's top restaurants. Comfort food dishes (such as meatloaf with mashed potatoes or fishcakes with Pommery mustard) are also excellent (see p87).

Top 10 Spots to Break your Diet

Finale
Try the molten chocolate gateau or rich crème brûlée.
§ 1 Columbus Ave • Map M5 • 30 Dunster St, Cambridge • Map B1

L. A. Burdick Chocolatiers
Sinful bon-bons and Boston's best hot chocolate. § 52D Brattle St, Cambridge • Map B1

Kickass Cupcakes
Cake-lover's heaven in a paper wrapper. § 378 Highland Ave, Somerville

ChocoLee Chocolates
Truffles and bon-bons by Lee Napoli. § 23 Dartmouth St • Map F6

Flour Bakery & Café
Delicious cakes, cookies, and cups of coffee. § 1595 Washington St • Map F6 • 12 Farnsworth St • Map R5

Sugar Heaven
"Penny candy" by the pound for childhood memories. § 669 Boylston St • Map L5

Eldo Cake House
Western-style iced cakes and Chinese treats. § 36 Harrison Ave • Map P4

Lizzy's Ice Cream
Chopped candy bars and sundae toppings in super-rich ice cream. § 31A Church St, Cambridge • Map B1

Langham Boston Chocolate Dessert Buffet
A delicious range of French chocolate pastry and sweets. § 250 Franklin St • Map Q4 • Open Sep–Jun: Sat

Christina's Homemade Ice Cream
Exotic spices and flavors add punch. § 1255 Cambridge St, Cambridge • Map D2

Note: Cafés serious about their coffee do not offer "flavored" coffees, but may offer a choice between light and dark roasts

Left Noir Right The Oak Long Bar & Kitchen

Bars

Drink
This trendy subterranean bar in the Fort Point district wins praise for its impressive lineup of classic and classically inspired cocktails. Knowledgeable bartenders may quiz you to create a drink to suit your character. House signature drink is the Fort Point variation on a Manhattan. ✪ 348 Congress St • Map R5 • 617 695 1806

Oak Long Bar & Kitchen
The Copley Plaza hotel bar serves a full roster of craft cocktails and a farm-to-table seasonal dining menu. In summer, drinks and meals can be enjoyed on the outdoor patio, which appropriately overlooks the twice-weekly farmers' market. ✪ 138 St James Ave • Map L6

Beer selection

Firebrand Saints
The neighborhood bar for MIT students and about half the dot-coms on the East Coast, Firebrand Saints is wildly original, right down to its light-projection streetscapes. Bar food ranging from porchetta sandwiches to poached lobster accompany the quirky alchemist cocktails. ✪ 1 Broadway, Cambridge •Map E3

Delux Café
The kind of place that is so unique, you want to keep it a secret. The South End's intimate Delux Café attracts a refreshing, one-of-a-kind mix of professionals, bike messengers, and gay boys and girls, all suckers for the bar's kitschy Elvis motif, extensive on-tap beers, and perpetual broadcast of the Cartoon Network (see p109).

Towne Stove & Spirits
While Towne wins rave reviews for its upscale comfort food, the drinks menu may be even better. An eclectic range of cocktails includes the likes of Back-Bacon Manhattan (bourbon, bitters, and bacon-infused vermouth). Less daring guests will also find plenty of classic cocktails to tingle their tastebuds. ✪ 900 Boyleston St • Map E5

Les Zygomates
The dinner crowd at Les Zygomates (the French term for the facial muscles that make you smile) is lured by reasonably priced French bistro fare. Come 9pm, the sleek, whimsically designed bar area comes alive with young professionals intent on flexing and making the most of their smile muscles and appreciating the nightly live jazz performances (see p111).

Hawthorne
This suave craft cocktail bar anchors the nightlife scene at the Hotel Commonwealth in Kenmore Square. Lounge-like in the front, cozy in the back, it's the place to drink and socialize.

Creative house cocktails push all the alchemist buttons and the first-rate wine list includes several sparkling wines by the glass. ◎ *500 Commonwealth Ave • Map D5*

Regattabar
The giants of jazz often stop at this nautical-themed lounge in Cambridge's Charles Hotel. Drinks may not be extraordinary but the talent is; past visitors have included McCoy Tyner, Ron Carter, and local favorite the Charlie Kolhase Quintet. A popular place, its shows sell out quickly *(see p124)*.

Noir
Sophisticated bar food such as flatbread pizzas, or chicken and shrimp skewers with dipping sauces, complement equally sophisticated variants on the martini. The all-black decor with high-backed banquettes creates a perfect atmosphere for private carrying-on. Waitresses carry flashlights to help read the menu. ◎ *Charles Hotel, 1 Bennet St. Cambridge • 617 661 8010 • Map B1*

Alibi
Set in the former drunk tank of the Charles Street Jail (now the posh Liberty Hotel), Alibi retains the bluestone floors and vestiges of the cell walls to form little nooks to lounge in while enjoying a drink or two. The outdoor patio is great for cocktails at sunset. ◎ *215 Charles St • Map F3*

Les Zygomates

Top 10 Locally Brewed Beers

1 Chamberlain Pale Ale
An English-style pale ale with the delicious, malty middle of its forebears.

2 Harpoon IPA
Ranked among the top domestic and imported India pale ales by *Beer Connoisseur Magazine*.

3 John Harvard's Nut Brown
Try this malty, light ale at John Harvard's Brew House (33 Dunster St, Cambridge).

4 Samuel Adams Octoberfest
Sam's finest – available only during the autumn – with deep amber coloring and a warm, spicy smoothness.

5 Boston Beer Works Fenway Pale Ale
Don your Red Sox cap and sip a light Fenway Pale at Beer Works *(see p116)*.

6 Samuel Adams Boston Lager
The beer that put Sam back on the brewing map after a 200-year hiatus.

7 Just Beer's Moby D
Dry-hopped American ale, available in bottles, is conveniently sold at both beer shops and wine shops.

8 Samuel Adams Cherry Wheat Ale
Like a hybrid between champagne and cherry soda; available at most liquor stores.

9 Harpoon UFO Hefeweizen
Unfiltered, Belgian-style brew, with fruity undertones.

10 Longfellow Winter Ale
Robust, strong ale for those cold winter nights (on tap October to April).

Note: *Unless otherwise specified, locally brewed beers listed here are available citywide*

Left **Johnny D's** Center **Royale** Right **Ryles**

TOP 10 Dance & Live Music Venues

Beehive
The nightly music mix here might sometimes veer to cabaret or even burlesque, but local jazz musicians are the mainstay for a usually well-dressed, mature crowd at least a decade past their schooldays. Convivial bar scene and some excellent comfort food, such as paella or polenta with ratatouille, round out the multi-faceted appeal of this great night out. ◈ *541 Tremont St • Map M6 • 617 423 0096*

The Middle East
The region's alternative rock scene can trace its genesis to this Central Square landmark. This influential venue has launched many careers. Seminal local bands like the Pixies, Mighty Mighty Bosstones, and Morphine all played on the Middle East's three stages. Today, the club continues the tradition, openly embracing musicians operating just under the mainstream, popular radar *(see p124)*.

House of Blues
The House of Blues chain was born across the river in Cambridge, and this 2,400-capacity room behind Fenway Park continues the commitment to American music: blues, gospel, jazz, rhythm & blues, and roots-based rock 'n' roll. A Gospel brunch is offered on Sundays, and the restaurant also opens during Red Sox evening home games. ◈ *215 Lansdowne St • Map D5 • 888 693 BLUE • Adm concert nights only*

Gypsy Bar
The sumptuous red interior, glam lighting, and extensive range of designer vodkas in the Gypsy Bar combine a stylish high-techno approach with enchanting, old-fashioned romanticism. It is easy to see why this attention-seekers' paradise has won various polls including sexiest bar and best pick-up spot *(see p109)*.

Whiskey Priest
An Irish gastropub located in a prime waterfront spot in the Fort Point district, Whiskey Priest has live acoustic music every Wednesday, karaoke on Thursday, DJs on Friday, and live rock bands on Saturday. An impressive menu of over 100 whiskeys is rounded off with a wide range of beers. The venue is convenient for the World Trade Center. ◈ *150 Northern Ave • Map H4 • 617 426 8111 • Free*

Scullers Jazz Club

Note: Nightlife and live music venues usually close at 1 or 2am

Ryles

6 One of Inman Square's greatest assets, where murals of Duke, Dizz, and Lady Day inspire top jazz bands to go, go, go. Call ahead to learn if samba or swing lessons are scheduled, and don't miss the good value Sunday jazz brunch: no cover, live jazz, boisterous crowds, and hearty entrées that rarely venture above $10. ⊕ *212 Hampshire St, Cambridge • Map D2 • 617 876 9330 • Closed Mon • Adm*

Royale

7 Housed in an ornate, bilevel theater, the Royale can accommodate more nightlife denizens than any other Boston club. Top 40, '80s, Latin, and house music are pumped through the powerful sound system, while a mixed crowd lounges around on cushy banquettes or keeps the beat on the mammoth dance floor *(see p109)*.

Sign, Ryles

Johnny D's

8 World-music aficionados and lovers of the eclectic from all over the city have been flocking here for years to hear live funk, zydeco, folk rock, blues, jazz, and international music. Reserve ahead for one of the 300 seats. The beat keeps going seven nights a week *(see p124)*.

Paradise Rock Club

9 Although no longer in its original downtown location, the Paradise is the oldest name in Boston rock venues. Icons from the '70s and '80s such as Van Halen, the Police, and Blondie first put the club on the map. Today, the Paradise remains true to its rock 'n' roll roots, welcoming nationally recognized acts that favor volume levels north of ten. ⊕ *967 Commonwealth Ave • Map C5 • 617 562 8800 • Adm*

Scullers

10 Enthusiastic champion of Latin jazz and emerging artists (for example, Norah Jones and Diana Krall started here), Scullers is a well-known venue for internationally established musicians. A great place to enjoy a drink and an evening of smooth jazz by some of the best performers in the business. ⊕ *400 Soldiers Field Rd • Map C4 • 617 562 4111 • Closed Sun & Mon • Adm*

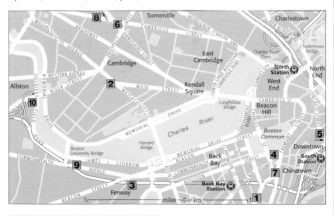

Left **Club Café** Right **Sign, Machine**

TOP 10 Gay & Lesbian Hang-Outs

Club Café

A video lounge and a popular Sunday brunch infallibly bring out the beautiful boys at this multifunction South End meeting spot. Choose from the casually elegant restaurant, which puts inspired twists on classic continental fare, the mirrored bar area – perfect for scoping the room – and the sleek cocktail lounge out the back. ◈ *209 Columbus Ave • Map M6*

Midway Café
Having offered its stage to rockabilly, punk, swing, reggae, and hip-hop acts since 1987, the Midway Café is partially responsible for Jamaica Plain's *(see p129)* youth-driven renaissance. Most nights bring an eclectic, edgy mix of music lovers, both gay and straight. The club's Thursday Women's Dance Night is the most popular lesbian club night in town.
◈ *3496 Washington St, Jamaica Plain • Adm*

Glamlife Thursdays
As if commanding the best lights, best sound, and best DJs in New England was not enough, Estate compels the finest gay men in the city to strut through its door every Thursday for five hours of serious dancing. Boston's longest running gay

club night brings in the world's leading circuit DJs, along with special guests like drag queen extraordinaire Lady Bunny.
◈ *1 Boylston Pl • Map N4 • 617 351 7000*

Fritz
With six flatscreen TVs positioned around this South End bar, there's no need to miss the action of any game, anywhere. Boston's premier gay and lesbian sports bar also fields its own local league basketball, softball, darts, and flag football teams. Afternoons can be relaxed, but count on fighting for a stool once the after-work crowd arrives. Located next door to the Chandler Inn, this is very much a traveler-friendly bar. ◈ *26 Chandler St • Map M6 • 617 482 4428*

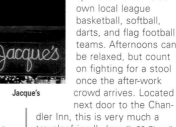

Jacque's

Jacque's Cabaret
One of the oldest names on the Boston gay club scene, Jacque's has been welcoming queer rock bands, drag queens, and their adoring fans long before being "out" was "in." Garage rock and beer fuel the downstairs scene, while up above you will find cabaret acts, rockers, and transvestites perform. Queens generally command the stage Tuesday through Friday and bands play mostly on weekends *(see p109)*.

Machine

6 Downstairs from its older brother Ramrod, Machine keeps things loose and relaxed. A billiard room, video games, and a comfy lounge area ensure plenty of diversions for gay men other than the pulsing, sunken dance-floor, and four bars. Male strippers often appear on Saturdays, supplying plenty of eye candy to supplement the beautiful crowd. ⌖ *1254 Boylston St • Map E5 • Adm*

Ramrod

7 On Saturday nights, club goers must wear black leather (no brown leather or suede, please), full Western wear (think John Travolta in *Urban Cowboy*) – or go shirtless. That's right, guys: without the gear there is no beer. Fortunately, the prohibitive dress code is well worth it, with weekend fetish shows and throbbing techno music. Ramrod is without a doubt Boston's oldest hardcore scene. ⌖ *1254 Boylston St • Map E5*

The Alley Bar

8 Harking back to closeted days, The Alley has a mellow, sociable vibe, with playful activities including karaoke, pool tournaments, underwear parties, and other theme nights for men who want to meet men. A big Alley attraction is the Saturday-night Bear Party for full-framed guys and those who love them. There is an upstairs/downstairs set-up which separates the various theme night crowds from local drinkers. ⌖ *14 Pi Alley, Cambridge • Map G4 • 617 263 1449*

Glamlife Thursdays

Paradise Bar

9 This Kendall Square club is best known for having live male dancers six nights a week, and for fielding new amateur talent. The upstairs bar shows big-screen movies (gay porn after 10pm), while the downstairs room is a dance hall – no high heels allowed. ⌖ *180 Massachusetts Ave, Cambridge • Map D3 • 617 868 3000*

Boston Eagle

10 A doorway-mounted wooden eagle has welcomed gay men to this subterranean South End bar for years. Having no qualms about simply being a gay bar, the Eagle is not a place to dance. The dimly lit bar area is roomy and comfortable; in the back, a mirrored wall captures pool sharks and pinball wizards at work. ⌖ *520 Tremont St • Map F6*

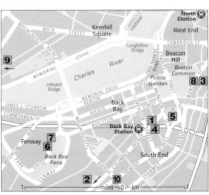

Left **Somerville Theatre** Center **Hatch Shell** Right **Concert, Symphony Hall**

🔟 Performing Arts Venues

1 Symphony Hall
Opened in 1900, Symphony Hall is one of the world's most acoustically perfect concert venues (it is a National Historic Landmark) and is the the home of the internationally renowned Boston Symphony Orchestra. The BSO commissions many new works, performs US and world premieres, and also frequently welcomes sought-after guest conductors and soloists. ❧ 301 Massachusetts Ave • Map E6 • 617 266 1492 • www.bso.org

2 Wang Theatre
Capturing the gilded and marbled opulence of its muse, Versailles, the 3,600-seat Wang ranks among the city's most beautiful buildings. The Wang hosts touring productions from Broadway and London's West End as well as dance and opera productions by local companies. ❧ 270 Tremont St • Map N5 • 617 482 9393 • www.citicenter.org

Detail, Wang Theatre

3 Hatch Shell
The Esplanade's biggest attraction is this semi-enclosed concert venue. Every July 4th (see p54) the Boston Pops orchestra rings in Independence Day here. Free Friday Flicks brings family faves such as *The Wizard of Oz* to the screen, while dance and music events occur almost nightly during summer. ❧ The Esplanade • Map M3 • 617 635 4505

4 Boston Center for the Arts
Home to four resident theater companies, four stages (including Boston's first new theater in 75 years), and a gallery, the BCA is the cornerstone of the South End arts scene. The artists who perform and exhibit here present work as provocative as you might find in New York. ❧ 539 Tremont St • Map F5 • 617 426 5000 • www.bcaonline.org

5 Sanders Theatre
Located in Harvard's splendid Memorial Hall (see p19), this theater has hosted many luminaries over its 120 plus years. Great performers of the past century have graced its intimate stage, including mime artist Marcel Marceau, and Longfellow, Oliver Wendell Holmes, and Ralph Wardo Emerson were among its early audiences. ❧ 45 Quincy St, Cambridge • Map B1 • 617 496 2222

6 New England Conservatory, Jordan Hall
Dozens of local orchestral and choral ensembles call the NEC's Jordan Hall home. Built at the turn of the 20th century and renowned for its intimacy and impressive acoustics, the space is listed on the National Registry of Historic Landmarks. The New England Conservatory presents more than 450 free concerts a year, and hosts ticketed events by other

Five Week Singers, Berklee Performance Center

music organizations. ◈ *30 Gainsborough St • Map E6 • 617 585 1260 • www.nccmusic.edu*

Loeb Drama Center
Harvard's Loeb Drama Center trains the university's performing arts students and houses one of New England's best theater companies, the American Repertory Theatre. The ART presents unorthodox stagings of Shakespeare, work by up-and-coming playwrights, and spirited plays for children. ◈ *64 Brattle St, Cambridge • Map B1 • 617 547 8300 • www.amrep.org*

ImprovAsylum
Expect a party just as much as a performance at this North End favorite. Public participation is an integral part of the Improv's frenetically paced productions, which usually leave the audience applauding raucously. ◈ *216 Hanover St • Map Q2 • 617 263 6887*

Berklee Performance Center
Berklee, the world's largest independent music college, boasts this premier venue. The great acoustics ensure that some of the most highly distinguished jazz, folk, and world musicians play here. ◈ *136 Massachusetts Ave • Map J6 • 617 266 7455 • www.berkleebpc.com*

Somerville Theatre
Extensive renovation has returned this Davis Square landmark to its original, ornate glory. When it isn't hosting some of the country's finest jazz, world music, and underground rock acts, the Somerville packs audiences in for great value, second-run movies. ◈ *55 Davis Sq, Somerville • 617 625 5700*

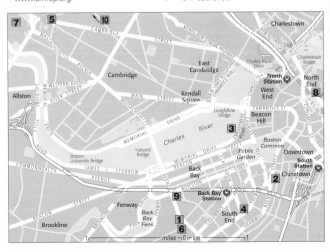

For more on Boston's Theater District **See pp104–111**

Left **Fourth of July** Right **First Night**

🔟 Festivals & Events

Fourth of July

Given Boston's indispensable role in securing independence for the original 13 colonies, Independence Day adopts a certain poignancy here. With beer-fueled barbecues and a fireworks display on the Charles River banks, Boston throws the nation a rousing birthday party.

Chinese New Year

Chinatown *(see pp104–11)* buzzes with the pageantry of the Chinese New Year during January to March. Streets are transformed into patchworks of color, while sidewalk vendors peddle steamed buns, soups, and other Chinese delights. Don't miss the annual parade, held the Saturday following the Lunar New Year.

New England Flower Show

For one week in March, more than 150,000 visitors descend on this indoor exhibition, hosted at various venues, to forget their winter blues and enjoy the spectacular display of bright blooms and fragrant aromas.

First Night

Despite the possibility of staggeringly cold weather, the New Year's Eve festivities remain among the most highly anticipated events of Boston's year. A

pass grants access to concerts, performances, and museum exhibits throughout the city at a reasonable price, not to mention a dazzling midnight fireworks display over Boston harbor.

Cambridge River Festival

For one day in mid-June the banks of the Charles River in Cambridge host a celebration of the city's lively and diverse population. Musicians and dancers perform and artists sell their wares. Food vendors offer a taste of home.

Plaque celebrating Boston Marathon

Feast of St. Anthony

The Feast of St. Anthony caps an entire summer of feast holidays in the North End *(see pp90–95)*. On the last weekend in August, from morning well into the night, Hanover Street bulges with revelers, parades, and food vendors giving a vibrant display of the area's old-world Italian spirit.

St. Patrick's Day

Boston's immense Irish-American population explains why few, if any, American cities can match Boston's Irish pride. Come Paddy's Day, pubs host live Irish bands and increasingly raucous crowds. The South Boston St. Patrick's Day Parade, with its famous drum corps, is a tradition that starts off from Broadway "T" station.

Note: Contact the Boston Convention & Visitors Bureau for information on festivals and events (1 888 733 2678; www.bostonusa.com)

August Moon Festival

In mid-August, Chinatown *(see pp104–11)* commemorates the summer's fullest moon – signifying the beginning of the harvest season – with a jubilant, unique festival. A dragon dance snakes through the area and vendors line the streets hawking everything from hand-painted fans and herbal remedies to the festival's official food, the semisweet mooncake.

Boston Restaurant Week

For one to two weeks in March and August more than 100 restaurants in Boston, Cambridge, and neighboring suburbs offer bargain, fixed-price lunch and dinner menus. Locals look forward to the opportunity to sample new restaurants, so it is wise to make reservations.
❧ www.restaurantweekboston.com

Lilac Sunday

While the Arnold Arboretum *(see p127)* counts 4,463 species of flora, one plant deserves particular celebration. When its 500 lilac plants are at their fragrant, color-washed peak, garden enthusiasts arrive in droves for a May Sunday of picnics, folk dancing, and tours of the lilac collections.

August Moon Festival

Top 10 Sporting Traditions

Boston Marathon
The country's oldest marathon beckons sports lovers.
❧ 3rd Mon/Apr • 617 236 1652

Head of the Charles Regatta
Rowing crews race down the Charles while the banks teem with boisterous onlookers.
❧ 3rd Sat & Sun/Oct • 617 868 6200

Red Sox vs Yankees
The most heated rivalry in US sports flares up every time the Yanks visit Fenway Park *(see p113)*. ❧ 617 267 1700

Boston Celtics
The Celts keep basketball playoff dreams alive at TD Garden. ❧ 617 624 1000

Boston Bruins
Crowds cheer this ice hockey team at the TD Garden. ❧ 617 624 1000

Patriots
Gillette Stadium is the home of the Patriots, the winners of three Super Bowls in four years. ❧ 1 800 543 1776

Harvard vs Yale
These Ivy League football toughs butt helmets at Harvard Stadium every other fall.
❧ 617 495 3454

Beanpot Hockey Tournament
Every February Boston's top collegiate hockey teams play each other at the TD Garden.
❧ 617 624 1000

The Revolution
The state's entry in Major League Soccer is an annual playoff threat at the Gillette Stadium. ❧ 1 800 543 1776

New Year's Plunge
Every Jan 1, since 1904, the L Street Brownies take a plunge in Boston Harbor.

Note: *For more information on events check local publications such as* Boston Phoenix *or* Boston Globe

Left & Center **Stores, Newbury Street** Right **Stall, Faneuil Hall Marketplace**

Essential Shopping Experiences

1 Newbury Street
Try as it might, Back Bay's most famous street cannot escape comparisons to Beverly Hills' Rodeo Drive. True, both offer stupendous people-watching, sophisticated shopping, chic dining, and prestigious galleries. Yet, with its 19th-century charm and convenient subway stops, Newbury Street outclasses its built-yesterday Left Coast counterpart by far. *See pp80–9.*

Red Sox Team Store

2 Red Sox Team Store
With World Series titles dating back to 1903 and the oldest ballpark in professional baseball, the Boston Red Sox engender a fan loyalty matched by few other teams. This memorabilia shop, across the street from Fenway Park *(see p113)*, sells every permutation of hat, jersey, and T-shirt imaginable, as well as signed bats, balls, and gloves. It also has baseball cards for hardcore collectors, while limited-edition bobbleheads make a quirky gift. ◈ *19 Yawkey Way • Map D5*

3 Charles Street
Charm abounds on this bluest of blue-blooded street, which is studded with antique dealers *(see p78)*, specialty grocers, and modern houseware boutiques. Come nightfall, wrought-iron gas lamps illuminate the brick sidewalks, residents hurry home with wine and fresh flowers, and sleek bistros buzz with excitement. ◈ *Map M3*

4 Artists' Open Studios
Boston's visual artists open their studios to the public on selected spring and fall weekends. Boston's numerous studio events are mostly in converted former warehouses. One of the most popular is the South End Open Studio event. Start at the Boston Center for the Arts *(see p52)* where there are many studios nearby and pick up a map for the rest. ◈ *www.cityofboston.com*

5 Garment District
The vintage clothing and bargain-priced trends of the Garment District are every Boston hipster's retort to fashion. Fancy-dress costumes are found on the first floor, but the best deal happens every morning when the shop snips open a vast bale of clothes to sell by the pound. ◈ *200 Broadway, Cambridge • Map D2*

6 Copley Place
This was among the country's first upscale urban shopping

malls. It counts such *du mode* tenants as Louis Vuitton, Tiffany, Neiman Marcus, and Coach. Footwear addicts are fond of Stuart Weitzman and Jimmy Choo boutiques. ✆ *100 Huntington Ave • Map L6*

The Haymarket

Being presented with a grilled salmon fillet may be more appealing than cooking one yourself, but this 350-year-old outdoor produce market still holds undeniable charm for visitors. Witness the feeding frenzy as fishmongers try to undercut each other on the day's catch. ✆ *Map Q2 • Open noon–7pm Fri, 7am–7pm Sat*

Harvard Square Bookstores

Harvard Square's bookstores are some of the most distinguished in the country. The Harvard Coop boasts 170,000-plus titles, while Schoenhof's Foreign Books specializes in non-English books. The c.1932 Harvard Book Store (1256 Massachusetts Ave) stocks countless new and used titles. And the irrepressible Revolution Books *(see p122)* keeps the red flag waving with socialist and communist literature. ✆ *Map B1*

Fish stall, The Haymarket

Faneuil Hall Marketplace

With its millions of visitors every year, Faneuil Hall Marketplace would not be found on any best-kept secret list. However, with its central location, rich colonial history, and plethora of food stalls, it offers a unique shopping experience. Choose from name-brand stores such as Victoria's Secret or the more unusual offerings in the fleet of pushcarts. See pp12–13.

SoWa Open Market

Expect clothing, jewelry, and art at Boston's art and indie design market, held every Sunday in the South End. A farmers' market augments the summer scene as top Boston food trucks feed hungry shoppers. ✆ *465 Harrison Ave • Map G6*

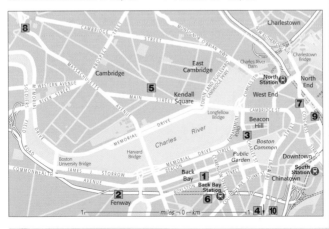

Left **Biking the Emerald Necklace** Right **People-watching in the Public Garden**

🔟 Boston Pastimes

1 People-watching on Boston Common

Corralled by bustling, commercial Tremont Street, stately Beacon Street, and genteel Charles Street, Boston Common lies at the confluence of three disparate worlds. Whatever the season, a stroll through the common yields a veritable cross section of the city's residents. *See pp14–15.* **Rollerblading**

2 Pilgrimage to Revere Beach

The first hot day of summer sparks a massive northbound migration via the MBTA blue line to the popular Revere Beach *(see p71).* Salsa music blares from passing cars on Ocean Avenue, soccer players stake out their pitches, and sun worshippers jostle for space at the shore break. 🅢 *Revere Beach Blvd, Revere*

3 Second-guessing the Red Sox

As soon as their baseball team opens spring training in March, Red Sox fans fill the talk-show airwaves with vehement assaults on the skills and intelligence of the manager. If the Sox lead the league in October, the manager is hailed as a genius. If they fall short, there's no place to hide. *See p113.*

4 Summer Sundays on Memorial Drive

Closed to vehicular traffic on summer Sundays, Cambridge's twisting, riverside Memorial Drive becomes a blur of rollerbladers, bicyclists, and joggers. 🅢 *Rent a bicycle at Cambridge Bicycle* • *259 Massachusetts Ave, Cambridge* • *617 876 6555*

5 Biking the Emerald Necklace

Taking in all 6 miles (9.5 km) of the Emerald Necklace *(see p15)* is best accomplished on a bicycle. The well-maintained trails lead riders from the wooded environs of Arnold Arboretum *(see p127)* to the Back Bay Fens *(see p113)* and onward to the Public Garden *(see pp14–15).* 🅢 *Rent wheels from Urban Adventours* • *103 Atlantic Ave* • *617 670 0637*

6 Boating on the Charles

Dawn on the Charles River Basin sees local rowing crews taking advantage of the water's glass-smooth stillness. By late

Sailboats, Charles River

morning, a breeze kicks up, beckoning fleets of small sailboats. When the wind diminishes toward sunset, canoeists arrive to enjoy the water's renewed calm.

Skating on the Frog Pond

Few scenes capture quintessential Boston better than a snow-covered Boston Common (see pp14–15) with figures twirling and sliding on the Frog Pond ice Rent some skates and partake in the scene, then refuel in the cozy warming hut. ◈ Open mid-Nov–mid-Mar: 10am–4pm Mon, 10am–9pm Tue–Thu & Sun, 10am–10pm Fri & Sat

Watching Quincy Market Street Performers

Even if you've had lunch and shopped until your shoe soles are worn out, a trip to Faneuil Hall Marketplace (see pp12–13) is worthwhile if only to watch the street performances. Jugglers, magicians, and other acts are surrounded by crowds of onlookers, all rapt with amazement and amusement.

Tango by Moonlight

For five or six summer nights, the Tango Society brings a bit of Buenos Aires to the Weeks Foot Bridge (see p63), inviting some 200 couples to summon the passion within and dance the tango from moonrise 'til midnight. ◈ Check www.bostontango.org

Sampling the Food Truck Specialties

Boston's food trucks are the ultimate movable feast, cooking up everything from crêpes to lobster rolls, barbecue to tacos. One of the best places to check out the offerings and enjoy an alfresco meal is along the Rose Kennedy Greenway recreation path that has replaced an elevated highway.

Top 10 Beaches

Revere Beach
An old-fashioned boardwalk, lively crowds, and great Boston views. See p71.

Duxbury Beach
An uncrowded South Shore jewel with soft white sands. ◈ Canal St, Duxbury

Crane Beach
Five miles (8 km) of coastline with gentle waves and rolling dunes. See p71.

Singing Beach
Gorgeous blue waters, rocky outcrops, and a picture-perfect beach town. ◈ Beach St, Manchester-by-the-Sea

Constitution Beach
Family friendly, with clean sand, picnic areas, lifeguards, and great Boston views. ◈ Bennington St, East Boston

Carson Beach
Clean facilities, lifeguards, and kayak rentals. ◈ William J. Day Blvd, South Boston

L Street Beach
Home of the "L Street Brownies," famous for their Jan 1 plunge at this South Boston landmark. ◈ William J. Day Blvd, South Boston

Malibu Beach
Hardly a match for its Left Coast namesake, but popular for swimming as well as tennis and basketball courts. ◈ Morrissey Blvd, Dorchester

Pleasure Bay Beach
Enclosed by a man-made causeway; there are no waves, but clean sand, water, and facilities. ◈ Old Harbor Reservation, Day Blvd, South Boston

Wollaston Beach
Boston Harbor's longest beach has clean sand and facilities attracting South Shore families. ◈ Quincy Shore Dr, Quincy

Note: For more information on beaches, contact the Depa… of Conservation and Recreation: 617 626 1250

Left **Boston Duck Tours** Center **Children's Museum** Right **Franklin Park Zoo**

⑩ Activities for Children

1 Boston Duck Tours

Board a refurbished, World War II-era, amphibious vehicle that plies the Charles River waters as smoothly as it navigates Back Bay streets. This historic tour encompasses all the peninsula and is conducted by courteous drivers and informative, entertaining guides who are great at keeping kids engaged. *Prudential Center and Museum of Science • Map K6 • 617 267 3825 • Open mid-Mar–Nov: 9am–dusk daily • Adm • www.bostonducktours.com*

2 Children's Museum

This venerable funhouse pioneered the interactive-exhibit concept now found in museums worldwide and is a real blast for kids and parents. It includes a climbing wall, a Big Dig-style *(see p37)* construction zone, and a science playground where tracks, balls, and bubbles make learning fun. *300 Congress St • Map R5 • 617 426 6500 • Open 10am–5pm daily, to 9pm Fri • Adm • www.boston childrensmuseum.org*

3 Swan Boats

If Boston were to have a mascot, it would most likely sport white feathers and a graceful, arching neck. The swan boats have been a Public Garden *(see p15)* fixture since the first fleet glided onto the garden's shimmering pond in 1877. *Public Garden • Map N4 • 617 522 1966 • Open mid-Apr–mid-Sep: usually 10am–5pm daily • Adm*

4 Museum of Science

Hands-on learning exhibits, like assembling animal skeletons or building a computer model, teach children about scientific discovery. The Omni Theater thrills with its fast-paced IMAX projections, while the planetarium places the cosmos within reach. *Science Park • Map F2 • 617 723 2500 • Open 9am–9pm Fri, 9am–5pm Sat–Thu (Jul–Sep: 9am–9pm Sat–Thu) • Adm • www.mos.org*

5 New England Aquarium

The aquarium goes to great lengths to keep kids engaged through a variety of interactive displays. Nothing illustrates this better than the Edge of the Sea exhibit, where children can touch some of the region's typical tidepool dwellers. *See pp32–3.*

6 Fenway Park

For children with even the slightest interest in sports, a Red Sox game at legendary Fenway Park *(see p113)* is pure magic. Fans always feel part of the action at the country's most intimate professional baseball park. The peanut, hot dog, and soda vendors keep kids' enjoyment – and blood sugar levels – elevated. *4 Yawkey Way • Map D5 • 617 267 1700 • Check www.redsox. com for schedule*

Museum of Science

Prudential Skywalk

Located on the 50th floor of the Prudential Tower *(see p82)*, this observatory provides a rewarding Boston geography lesson. Should the jaw-dropping, 360-degree views not keep the youngsters enthralled, the audio/video tours of Boston's neighborhoods will. The swift, ear-popping elevator ride to the top is also a thrill. ⊗ *800 Boylston St • Map K6 • 617 859 0648 • open Mar–Oct: 10am–10pm daily; Nov–Feb: 10am–8pm daily • Adm*

Frog Pond

The Frog Pond makes children feel like protagonists in a quaint picture book. As soon as temperatures dip below freezing, kids flock to the pond for ice skating and hot chocolate at the adjacent warming hut. Boston's oft-oppressive summer days lure them back for splashing and frivolity beneath the central fountain. ⊗ *Boston Common • Map M4*

Street Entertainment

The best part of a visit to Faneuil Hall Marketplace is that you never know who – or what – you will see. "Benjamin Franklin" might administer a quick colonial

Museum of Science

history quiz to an unsuspecting child, a juggler might ask another to participate in a performance, or a street musician might stick the mic in a child's hand for a singsong. *See pp12–13.*

Franklin Park Zoo

Boston's urban zoo, dating back to 1913, houses over 200 species of animals. Its Tropical Forest section boasts gorillas, leopards, tropical birds, and many other exotic creatures. Bird's World consists of a free-flight cage holding dozens of species. The small, petting zoo allows kids to get up close and personal with animals of the decidedly huggable kind. ⊗ *1 Franklin Park Rd, Dorchester • 617 541 5466 • open 10am–5pm Mon–Fri, 10am–6pm Sat–Sun (Oct–Mar: 10am–4pm daily) • Adm • www.zoonewengland.com*

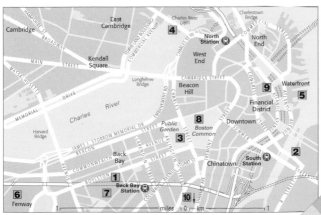

For tips on traveling with children **See p139**

Left **Long Wharf** Right **No Name Restaurant, Fish Pier**

🔟 Waterfront Areas

1 The Esplanade
Provided the Charles River Basin has not frozen over, collegiate rowing crews, canoeists, small sailboats, and the occasional coast guard patrol all share the waters off the Esplanade. Find a bench facing the water and take in the scene. ✪ *Map M3*

2 Castle Island Reservation
Connected to the mainland via an earthen causeway and crowned by the c.1851 Fort Independence, Castle Island is New England's oldest continually fortified site *(see p128)*. Aside from exploring the fort's bunkers and tunnels (in season), visitors enjoy fine panoramic views of Boston Harbor. ✪ *38 Taylor St, Dorchester • 617 727 5290*

3 Constitution Beach
Views of Downtown don't get much better than those from this tastefully revitalized beach and park area in East Boston. A clean beach, picnic areas, and lifeguards make this a favorite with families. ✪ *Bennington St, East Boston*

4 Fort Point Channel
Fort Port has lured artists to the neighborhood with affordable studio space in old warehouse buildings. Open studios in May and October offer a peek inside and a chance to bag a bargain on artwork. Where artists go, gentrification is sure to follow: the neighborhood now boasts the $300-million Federal Courthouse and trendy cafés and restaurants. ✪ *Map H5*

5 Fish Pier
By 1926 – 12 years after its construction – the Greco-Roman style Commonwealth Pier (aka Fish Pier) had become the world's busiest and largest fish market. The day's catch is still brought to the early-morning market here. Sample some of it in hearty chowders at the legendary No Name Restaurant *(see p42)*.

6 Long Wharf
The modern Marriott Hotel masks Long Wharf's 300 years of indispensability to Boston's merchant industry. Given its deep frontage and proximity to waterfront warehouses, the biggest ships of their day could dock here. Today, ferry services and cruise vessels depart from the wharf, creating a spirited dock scene. ✪ *Map R2*

The Esplanade

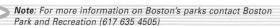

Note: *For more information on Boston's parks contact Boston Park and Recreation (617 635 4505)*

Rowes Wharf

7 Framed by the colossal atrium of the Boston Harbor Hotel *(see p146)*, Rowes Wharf is a popular docking spot for the high-end harbor cruise outfits and is a luxurious contrast to the city's grittier, saltier working docks. The hotel sponsors free concerts and film screenings on summer evenings. ◈ Map R3

Christopher Columbus Park

Christopher Columbus Park

8 Featuring an Italian marble sculpture of the seafaring Genoan, Christopher Columbus Park is among the North End's best-kept secrets. Vine-encrusted arches, manicured gardens, and sweeping harbor and skyline views make this a place to linger. ◈ Map P2

Puopolo Park

9 North End's Puopolo Park boasts supreme frontage on the harbor, looking out toward Charlestown. On warm days, the neighborhood's old guard enjoys a game of *bocce* (bowls). Nearby, kids play baseball or splash around in the outdoor pool. ◈ Map H2

Charles River Locks & Dam

10 The Charles River Dam controls water levels in the basin below and maintains separation of the river from the harbor. A series of locks permits boats to pass from one body of water to the other. Call for tour schedule. ◈ Map F2 • 617 727 1188 (ext. 445)

Top 10 Views

1 Prudential Skywalk
Jaw-dropping panoramic views from a 50th-floor observatory. See p61.

2 Longfellow Bridge
The entire Charles River Basin becomes your oyster on the "T" between Kendall and Charles/MGH stops. ◈ Map M2

3 Bunker Hill Monument
Climb to the capstone to see all of Charlestown, Cambridge, and Boston laid out before you. See p30.

4 Spirit of Boston Cruises
Ply the harbor waters and enjoy unrivaled city views. ◈ World Trade Center • 066 310 2469

5 Charlestown Bridge
Splendid harbor and Downtown vistas. ◈ Map G2

6 John J. Moakley Courthouse Park
This beautiful waterfront park has fine views of the towering Financial District.

7 Hyatt Regency Cambridge
Gaze across the Charles River from the hotel's Zephyr Lounge. ◈ 575 Memorial Drive, Cambridge • Map C4 • 617 492 1234

8 Weeks Foot Bridge
Prime spectator spot during the Head of the Charles Regatta *(see p55)*. ◈ Map B2

9 Dorchester Heights Monument
This colonial-style spire offers dizzying views of the city from its cupola.

10 Harborside Hyatt Hotel
The Hyatt's Harborside Grill and Patio boasts panoramic Boston views. ◈ 101 Harborside Drive, East Boston • 617 568 1234

Following pages **Boston Harbor**

Left **Peddocks Island** Right **View of Deer Island from Georges Island**

Boston Harbor Islands

Georges Island

As the terminal for the harbor islands ferry and water shuttles to other islands, Georges Island is the gateway to the Boston Harbor Islands National Park Area, which includes 34 islands enclosed within the curve of Boston Harbor. Visitors can hike, swim, explore historic buildings, view birds, and watch passing ships. But it is worth spending time here to view the massive remains of Civil War-era Fort Warren and check out the snack bar and gift shop. ⊛ *Islands open May–Oct (information booth at Long Wharf), 617 223 8666, www.bostonislands.org*

Grape & Bumpkin Islands

Both these islands are naturalist's delights – Bumpkin for its wildflowers, raspberries, and bayberries, Grape for its wild roses and bird life. On Bumpkin Island, hiking trails pass the ruins of a farmhouse and 19th-century children's hospital, which also housed German prisoners rescued from Boston Harbor in World War I.

Lovells Island

Known for its extensive dunes, Lovells also has an unsupervised swimming beach. Extensive hiking trails lead across dunes and through woodlands. The remains of Fort Standish, which was active during the Spanish American War and World War I, can also be explored.

Peddocks Island

Peddocks is one of Boston Harbor's largest and most diverse islands. Hiking trails circle a pond, salt marsh, and coastal forest, and pass by Fort Andrews, which was active in harbor defense from 1904 through to World War II. The island is known for the beach plums and wild roses which bloom profusely in the dunes. A visitor center and camping facilities make it an overnight destination.

Deer Island

Accessed by a causeway attaching the island to the mainland, 60 acres (24 ha) of the island were opened in 2006 for recreation and walking – with dramatic views of the Boston skyline. Deer Island is also known for its impressive, state-of-the-art $3.8 billion sewage treatment plant. Distinguished by 12 gigantic egg-shaped digesters, it was key to cleaning up Boston Harbor.

Fort Warren, Georges Island

Note: May–Oct ferries sail from Long Wharf to Georges Island where there's a shuttle service to other islands (call 617 223 8666)

Spectacle Island

Vastly enlarged by fill from the Big Dig (see p37), Spectacle Island has some of the highest peaks of the harbor islands and the best Boston skyline view. The construction of a café and visitor center has made it one of the most popular of the harbor islands. Visitors enjoy 5 miles (8 km) of trails and swimming beaches with lifeguards.

Little Brewster Island

Boston Light, the first US lighthouse, was constructed here in 1716 and it remains the last staffed offshore lighthouse in the country. Limited tours visit the small museum and lead visitors up the 76 spiral steps and two ladders to reach the top. ✎ *Island accessible by tour only: mid-Jun–late Sep: Fri–Sun • call for schedule • Reservations essential: 617 223 8666 • Adm*

Boston Light, Little Brewster Island

Gallops Island

Once the site of a popular summer resort, Gallops also served as quarters for Civil War soldiers, including the Massachusetts 54th Regiment (see p14). The island has an extensive sandy beach, a picnic area, hiking paths, and historic ruins of a former quarantine and immigration station. The Massachusetts Department of Conservation and Recreation has closed the island indefinitely for a thorough environmental clean up.

Thompson Island

A learning center since the 1830s, Thompson is the site of an Outward Bound program serving more than 5,000 students annually. The island's diverse geography includes rocky and sandy shores, a large salt marsh, and a hardwood forest. Killdeer, herons, and shorebirds abound. ✎ *Open Jun–Aug: Sat & Sun • 617 328 3900 • Ferries depart from EDIC Pier on Summer Street • Jul–Aug: Sat & Sun • Adm*

World's End

This 244-acre (99-ha) peninsula overlooking Hingham Bay is a geological sibling of the harbor islands, with its two glacial drumlins, rocky beaches, ledges, cliffs, and both salt- and freshwater marshes. Frederick Law Olmsted laid out the grounds for a homestead development here in the late 19th century. The homes were never built, but paths, formal plantings, and hedgerows remain. World's End is accessed by road by driving through Hingham. ✎ *Operated by Trustees of Reservations: 1 781 740 6665 • Adm to non-members*

Note: Islands are open 9am to sunset daily, closed in winter. Camping is allowed on Grape, Bumpkin, Peddocks, and Lovells by special permit

67

Left **Old Sturbridge Village** Right **Elms Mansion, Newport**

🔟 Day Trips: Historic New England

1 Lexington

Peaceful, leafy Lexington Green marks the first encounter of British soldiers with organized resistance by American revolutionaries. The rebels fortified their courage with a night of drinking at the adjacent Buckman Tavern (1 Bedford St). 🕲 *Massachusetts • Route 2 • Visitor information: 1875 Massachusetts Ave; 1 781 862 1450 • www.lexingtonchamber.org*

2 Concord

Rebels put the Redcoats to rout at North Bridge, Concord's main revolutionary battle site. This historical town was also the epicenter of American literature in the mid-19th century. Visitors can tour the homes of writers Ralph Waldo Emerson (Cambridge Turnpike), Nathaniel Hawthorne (455 Lexington Rd), and Louisa May Alcott (399 Lexington Rd). Henry

Witch Museum, Salem

David Thoreau's woodland haunts at Walden Pond now feature hiking trails and a swimming beach. 🕲 *Massachusetts • Route 2 • Visitor information: 58 Main St; 1 978 369 3120 • www.concordchamberofcommerce.org*

3 New Bedford

During the 19th century, local sailors and whalers plundered the oceans of the world, enriching the port of New Bedford. The National Historic District preserves many of the fine buildings of the whaling era, while the Whaling Museum (18 Johnny Cake Hill) gives accounts of the enterprise. 🕲 *Massachusetts • Routes I-95 & I-195 • Visitor information: 33 William St; 1 508 996 4095 • www.nps.gov/nebe*

4 Salem

A witch may not have been killed in Salem since 1692, but witchcraft paraphernalia fills many stores, and several sites such as the Witch Museum (19 Washington Sq North) tell the tale of this dark episode. The city is more proud of its China Trade days (1780s–1880s), which are engagingly recounted on National Park walking tours. Visit the Peabody Essex Museum (East India Sq) to see the treasures sea captains brought home. 🕲 *Massachusetts • Route 1A • Visitor information: 2 New Liberty St; 1 978 740 1650 • www.nps.gov/sama*

5 Plymouth

The recreated historic village of Plimoth Plantation (137 Warren

Note: Peter Pan Bus Lines (800 343 9999) and MBTA commuter rail (617 222 3200) operate to many of these destinations from South Station

Ave) gives a full immersion in to the lives of the first English settlers in Massachusetts. At the harbor, tour the *Mayflower II* (State Pier). On Thanksgiving, the town celebrates its pilgrim heritage with a parade in period dress. 🕙 *Massachusetts • Routes 3 & 44 • Visitor information: 130 Water St; 1 508 747 7525 • www.see-plymouth.com*

Lowell
Lowell was the cradle of the US's Industrial Revolution, where entrepreneurs dug power canals and built America's first textile mills on the Merrimack River. The sites within the National Historical Park (246 Market St) tell the parallel stories of a wrenching transformation from agricultural to industrial lifestyle. A 1920s weave room still thunders away at Boott Cotton Mills Museum (115 John St). 🕙 *Massachusetts • Routes I-93, I-95, & 3 • Visitor information: 246 Market St; 1 978 970 5000 • Adm to Boott Cotton Mills Museum • www.nps.gov/lowe*

Old Sturbridge Village
Interpreters in period costume go about their daily lives in a typical 1830s New England village. This large living history museum has more than 40 buildings on 200 acres (83 ha). Get a sense of the era by visiting the village common, mill district, and the traditional family farm. 🕙 *Massachusetts • Routes I-90, 20, & 84 • Visitor Center: 380 Main St; 1 800 733 1830 • www.osv.org*

Portsmouth
Founded in 1623 as Strawbery Banke, the historic houses on Marcy Street document three centuries of city life from early settlement through 20th century immigration. Picturesque shops, pubs, and restaurants surround Market Square and line the waterfront, and the surrounding leafy streets boast fine examples of Federal architecture. 🕙 *New Hampshire • Routes 1 or I-95 • Visitor information: 500 Market St; 1 603 610 5510 • www.portsmouthchamber.org*

Providence
Providence is a great walking city: stroll Benefit Street's "mile of history" to see an impressive group of Colonial and Federal houses; or visit Waterplace Park with its pretty walkways along the Providence River. Atwells Avenue on Federal Hill is Providence's Little Italy, bustling with restaurants and cafés. 🕙 *Rhode Island • Routes 1 or I-95 • Visitor information: 1 Sabin St; 1 401 751 1177 • www.goprovidence.com*

Newport
A playground for the rich since the late 1860s. Many of the elaborate "cottages" built by 19th-century industrialists are open for tours, including Breakers (Ochre Point Ave). For natural beauty, hike the 3.6 mile (5.5 km) Cliff Walk overlooking Narragansett Bay and Easton's Beach. 🕙 *Rhode Island • Routes I-93, 24, & 114 • Visitor information: 23 America's Cup Ave; 1 401 845 9123 • www.gonewport.com*

Note: *Costumed re-enactors dramatize the 1775 Battle of Lexington and Concord each year on Patriots Day (the third Monday in April)*

69

Left **Crane Beach, Ipswich** Right **Gloucester**

🔟 Day Trips: The Seaside

1 Cape Ann

Thirty miles (48 km) north of Boston, the granite brow of Cape Ann juts defiantly into the Atlantic – a rugged landscape of precipitous cliffs and deeply cleft harbors. In Gloucester, the cape's main harbor, a waterfront statue and plaque memorialize the 10,000 local fishermen who have perished at sea since 1623, and the Cape Ann Museum (27 Pleasant St) displays some superb maritime paintings. The picturesque harborfront of adjacent Rockport is an artists' enclave and is lined with galleries. Ⓢ Routes I-95 & 127 • Visitor information: 33 Commercial St, Gloucester; 1 978 283 1601

2 Upper Cape Cod

The Upper Cape is tranquil and low-key. Watch the boats glide through Cape Cod Canal or take the Shining Sea bikeway from Falmouth village to Woods Hole. If it's beaches you're after, Sandwich's Sandy Neck has huge dunes and excellent bird-watching, but Falmouth's Surf Drive is best for swimmers and Old Silver Beach is tops for sunset views. Ⓢ Routes 3, 6, & 28

3 Mid Cape Cod

The Mid Cape tends to be congested, especially in the town of Hyannis. But the north shore can be peaceful, with amazing wildlife and stunning views, especially from Gray's Beach in Yarmouth. Warmer water

and sandy strands line the south side of Mid Cape, with especially good swimming in Harwich and Dennisport. There's also excellent canoeing and kayaking on the Bass River. Ⓢ Route 3, 6, & 28

4 Outer Cape Cod

Here you'll find some of the area's best beaches. The 40-mile (64-km) National Seashore offers great surfing at Coast Guard and Nauset Light, and the beaches of Marconi, Head of the Meadow, and Race Point all have dramatic dunes and great ocean swimming. The artist colonies of Wellfleet and Truro are worth a visit as is Provincetown, a fishing village turned gay resort. Ⓢ Routes 3 & 6 • www.nps.gov/caco

5 Martha's Vineyard

Ferries to the 100-sq-mile (160-sq-km) island stop at Vineyard Haven. From here it's a short drive to old-fashioned Oak Bluffs with its gingerbread cottages and historic carousel. Venture south to Edgartown and the magnificent 19th-century homes of the rich whaling captains. The

Martha's Vineyard

 Note: For more information on Cape Cod contact the Chamber of Commerce at 1 508 362 3225 or go to www.capecodchamber.org

nearby 3-mile (4.8-km) Katama Beach is also a magnet for sun worshipers. On the southwest of the island, Menemsha remains a picturesque fishing village and Aquinnah's cliffs offer dramatic hiking. ◈ *Routes 3 & 28 to Woods Hole • ferry to Vineyard Haven: 1 508 477 8600 • Visitor information: Beach Rd, Vineyard Haven; 1 508 693 0085 • www.mvy.com*

Nantucket Island

Nantucket's Whaling Museum tells the tale of the Quaker whalers who made Nantucket prosperous in the 19th century. The island has shed its Quaker past and now boasts trophy beach houses and million-dollar yachts. For sports, there's kayaking, casting for striped bass from Surfside Beach, or cycling to the former fishing village of Sconset with its rose-covered clifftop cottages. ◈ *Routes 3 & 6 to Hyannis • ferry to Nantucket: 1 508 477 8600 • Visitor information: Zero Main St, Nantucket; 1 508 228 1700*

Ipswich

Crane Beach in Ipswich is one of New England's most scenic beaches, with more than 4 miles (6.5 km) of white sand, warm water, and outstanding bird-watching. Also on the Crane Estate, you can visit Castle Hill mansion and its lovely Italianate gardens. ◈ *Routes 95, 128, & 133, or 1A • Visitor information: 36 South Main St; 1 978 356 8540 • www.ipswichma.com*

Newburyport

In the 19th century, Newburyport was a prosperous seaport. The grand three-story mansions along the High Street present a virtual case study in Federal architecture, while boutiques and antiques shops line downtown Merrimac, Water, and State streets. The Parker River National Wildlife Refuge on the adjacent Plum Island is one of the US's top bird-watching sanctuaries. ◈ *Route I-95 & 1 • Visitor information: 38R Merrimac St; 1 978 462 6680*

Revere Beach

Established in 1896, Revere Beach was the first public beach in the US. Thanks to a centennial restoration, it's also one of the best, with nearly 3 miles (4.5 km) of clean white sand and clear blue water. ◈ *Routes 1 & 1A • "T" station: Revere Beach/Wonderland*

Hampton & Rye Beaches

The New Hampshire coast just south of Portsmouth has extensive sandy beaches. Wallis Sands State Park is ideal for swimming but the best of the rocky overlooks is Rye's Ragged Point picnic area. The honky-tonk social scene, however, is at Hampton Beach. Odiorne Point State Park in Rye has picnic areas and walking trails. ◈ *Routes I-95, NH 101, & 1A • Visitor information: 160 Ocean Blvd, Hampton Beach; 1 603 926 8717 • www.hamptonbeach.org*

Note: *Bay State Cruise Co. operates a ferry to Provincetown (mid-May–mid-Oct) from the World Trade Center, Boston, 617 748 1428*

71

AROUND TOWN

BOSTON'S TOP 10

Left **Sign, African Meeting House** Center **Reliefs, Federal-style mansion** Right **Louisburg Square**

Beacon Hill

WITH ITS ELEGANT, *19th-century row houses, quaint grocers, pricey antique shops, and hidden gardens, Beacon Hill screams "old money" like no other area in Boston. That some of the city's most exorbitant apartment rentals can still be found here suggests it will remain an enclave of exclusivity for years to come. Yet throughout the 19th century and well into the 20th, this inimitably charming neighborhood was a veritable checkerboard of ethnicities and earning groups – segregated though they were. Little of Beacon Hill's diversity has survived its relatively recent gentrification, but visitors can still experience the neighborhood's myriad pasts inside its opulent mansions and humble schoolhouses, and along its enchanting cobblestone streets.*

TOP 10 Attractions

1. Massachusetts State House
2. Museum of African American History
3. Nichols House Museum
4. Louisburg Square
5. Harrison Gray Otis House
6. Appalachian Mountain Club Headquarters
7. Beacon Street
8. Boston Center for Jewish Culture
9. George Middleton House
10. Parkman House

Ivy-clad façade, Beacon Hill

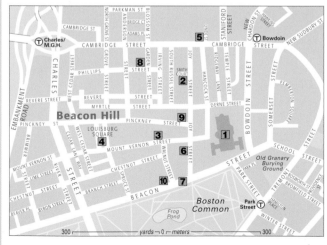

Note: *Massachusetts State House is situated on the Freedom Trail* See p8

1 Massachusetts State House

A 200-year-old codfish, a stained-glass image of a Native American in a grass skirt, and a 23-carat gold dome crowned with a pine cone – such are the curious eccentricities that distinguish Beacon Hill's most prestigious address *(see p11)*. ॐ *24 Beacon St • Map P3 • 617 727 3676 • Tours 10am–3:30pm Mon–Fri • Free (reservations recommended) • www.sec.state.ma.us/trs*

2 Museum of African American History

Based in the African Meeting House (the oldest extant black church in the US) and the adjoining Abiel Smith School (the nation's first publicly funded grammar school for African-American children) – the MAAH offers a look into the daily life of free, pre-Civil War African-Americans. The meeting house was a political and religious center for Boston's African-American community and it was here that abolitionists such as Frederick Douglass and William Lloyd Garrison delivered anti-slavery addresses in the mid-19th century. The museum has successfully preserved their legacy and that of countless others through workshops, exhibitions, and special events.

Drawing Room, Nichols House Museum

Senate Chamber, Massachusetts State House

ॐ *46 Joy St • Map N2 • 617 725 0022 • open 10am–1pm Mon–Sat • Adm • www.maah.org*

3 Nichols House Museum

An 1804 Charles Bulfinch design, 55 Mount Vernon is one of the earliest examples of residential architecture on Beacon Hill. Rose Nichols, the house's principal occupant for 75 years, bequeathed her home to the city as a museum, providing a glimpse of late 19th- and early 20th-century life on the Hill. A pioneering force for women in the arts and sciences, Nichols gained fame through her authoritative writings on landscape architecture and philanthropic projects. ॐ *55 Mount Vernon St • Map N3 • 617 227 6993 • open Apr–Oct: 11am–4pm Tue–Sat; Nov–Mar: 11am–4pm Thu–Sat • Adm*

4 Louisburg Square

Cobblestone streets, a genteel little gated park, and a hefty dose of Boston Brahmin cachet make this tight block of townhouses the city's most exclusive patch of real estate. Modeled after the traditional residential squares of London in 1826, the square was named in remembrance of the 1745 Battle of Louisburg in modern-day Quebec. ॐ *Map N3*

Dining Room, Harrison Gray Otis House

Harrison Gray Otis House

One of the principal developers of Beacon Hill, Harrison Gray Otis *(see p38)* served in the Massachusetts legislature and gained a reputation for living la dolce vita in this 1796 Bulfinch-designed manse. Like a post-Revolutionary Gatsby, Otis ensured his parties were the social events of the year. After falling into disrepair, the property was acquired in 1916 by the historical preservation society and restored to its original grandeur. *141 Cambridge St • Map N2 • 617 994 5920 • open 11am–4:30pm Wed–Sun • Adm • www.historicnewengland.org*

Appalachian Mountain Club Headquarters

The Appalachian Trail, or the A.T. as it is known to hiking cognoscenti, is America's premier walking path. Snaking through 2,168 miles (3,492 km) of pristine eastern wilderness – including 90 miles (145 km) in Massachusetts – the trail is maintained by members of the club. With a scale model of the trail, informative plaques on the walls, maps, guidebooks, and a knowledgeable staff, this is an essential stop for those planning a hike. *5 Joy St • Map N3 • 617 523 0636 • open 9am–5pm Mon–Fri • Free*

Beacon Street

Although it extends well beyond the Fenway, Beacon Street finds its true essence in the blocks between Park and Charles streets. Here it passes such highlights as the Boston Athenaeum, one of the oldest independent libraries in the country, the Massachusetts State House *(see p11)*, and the Bull and Finch Pub of *Cheers* TV fame. *Map N3*

Boston Center for Jewish Culture

The Vilna Shul testifies to the area's former vibrancy as Boston's first predominantly Jewish quarter. The congregation was founded in 1903 by immigrants who came from Vilna, Lithuania. The synagogue has become a center of Jewish culture with programs and exhibits. *13–18 Phillips St • Map N2 • 617 523 2324 • call for hours • www.vilnashul.com*

Boston Center for Jewish Culture

George Middleton House

The oldest remaining private residence on Beacon Hill built by African-Americans is a highlight of the Black Heritage Trail. George Middleton, a revolutionary war veteran, commissioned the house's

Black Heritage Trail

By and large the Paul Reveres and John Adams of this world have monopolized the history books. As a refreshing counterpoint, the Black Heritage Trail posits that black Bostonians, despite their marginalized histories, have played an indispensable role in the city's development. The trail illustrates this point at every turn, taking visitors past the homes and businesses of some of Boston's most influential black Americans. Tours leave from Faneuil Hall daily in summer, Mon–Sat in winter. Call 24 hours in advance for times and to book (617 742 5415; www. nps.gov/boaf).

construction shortly after the war. Legend has it that Middleton commanded an all-black company dubbed the "Bucks of America." ➌ *5–7 Pinckney St • Map N3 • Closed to the public*

George Middleton House

10 Parkman House

George Parkman – once a prominent physician at Harvard Medical School – lived in this house during the mid-19th-century. In 1849, in one of the most sensationalized murder cases in US history, Parkman was killed by a faculty member over a financial dispute. Both the crime and its aftermath were grisly – in the ensuing trial dental records were entered as evidence for the first time. ➌ *33 Beacon St • Map N3 • Closed to the public*

Beacon Hill by Day

Morning

Take the "T" to the Charles St/Massachusetts General Hospital stop and exit onto Charles Street. Enjoy a light breakfast at **Panificio Bakery** (144 Charles St) where the scones and muffins are other-worldly. Then continue along Charles Street and turn right onto Beacon Street for a glimpse of the **Bull and Finch Pub** (No. 84) – the bar that inspired the TV show *Cheers*. Continue up Beacon to the **Massachusetts State House** *(see p11)* for a free 45-minute tour; times vary. Afterward, cross the road to the Shaw Memorial, where a National Park ranger-led **Black Heritage Trail** tour departs at noon during summer. The trail provides an excellent survey of the area's architectural styles as well as its black culture sites, and terminates at the **Museum of African American History** *(see p75)*.

Afternoon

Walk back down the hill to Charles Street for a fortifying late lunch. Weather permitting, stock up on fresh fruit, a crusty baguette, and a sampling of imported cheeses at the charming **Savenor's Market** (160 Charles St) and have a picnic on the Common *(see pp14–15)*. Or for inexpensive, diner-style American fare (meatloaf and fruit pies), check out the **Paramount** (44 Charles St). After lunch, peruse the sleek accessories, art, and design at **Good** (88 Charles St) and spend the rest of the afternoon browsing Charles Street's antique shops *(see p78)*. Round the day off with a pint at **Seven's Ale House** *(see p79)*.

Left **Antique flatware for sale** Right **Room with a Vieux**

🔟 Antique & Gift Shops

1 Room with a Vieux
Owner Jeff Diamond scours France for unique furniture and light fixtures, which span the centuries. High-end Art Deco furniture pieces, bedboards, and Louis XV mirrors are strong points. ✆ *20 Charles St • Map M3 • Closed Sun*

2 Eugene Galleries
This shop has an excellent and fascinating selection of antique books, maps, and prints, including many depicting the development and history of Boston through various periods. ✆ *76 Charles St • Map M3*

3 Upstairs Downstairs
This cozy shop places a refreshing emphasis on affordability and function. Everything from mahogany four-poster beds to *belle époque* opera glasses are on display. ✆ *93 Charles St • Map M3*

4 20th Century Limited
Vintage designer costume jewelry and estate jewelry are the main attractions here. But don't overlook the handsome 1950s barware, vintage clothing accessories, and other collectibles. ✆ *73 Charles St • Map M3*

5 Boston Antiques Company
Twelve dealers run this bi-level space filled with dozens of 19th-century Japanese woodblocks and Impressionist landscape paintings. ✆ *119 Charles St • Map M3*

6 Blackstones of Beacon Hill
This is the place to go for unique Boston-themed gifts such as *Make Way for Ducklings* pillows and ornaments, as well as high-quality Fenway Park mugs. ✆ *46 Charles St • Map M3*

7 Elegant Findings
This intimate shop specializes in museum-quality, hand-painted 19th-century porcelain from all over Europe. You'll also find marble statuary, exquisite linens, and period furniture. ✆ *89 Charles St • Map M3 • Closed Tue, Wed & Sun*

8 Marika's Antiques
Packed to its dusty rafters with oil paintings, tarnished silverware, and mismatched china – nothing quite beats that thrill of discovery you'll find here. ✆ *130 Charles St • Map M3 • Closed Sun & Mon*

9 Black Ink
Labelled "unexpected necessities" by the owners, merchandise here ranges from four-way rubber bands to Weck canning jars to rubber stamps (hence the name). Always funky, always fun. ✆ *101 Charles St • Map M3*

10 Beacon Hill Chocolates
Handmade boxes decorated with vintage Boston scenes are ideal for assembling a gift assortment of artisan chocolates. Don't miss the signature swirl of Caramel Sushi. ✆ *91 Charles St • Map M3*

 Note: Unless otherwise specified, antique shops are open Mon–Sat (10 or 11am to 5 or 6pm) and Sun (noon–6pm)

Price Categories

For a three course meal for one with half a bottle of wine (or equivalent meal), taxes, and extra charges.	**$** under $30
	$$ $30–$45
	$$$ $45–$60
	$$$$ $60–$75
	$$$$$ over $75

Left **Bin 26 Enoteca**

🔟 Restaurants & Bars

1 Mooo
Mooo specializes in extraordinary beef and classic accompaniments at expense-account prices. Wine list includes many stellar names. ◈ 15 Beacon St • Map P3 • 617 670 2515 • $$$$$

2 Bin 26 Enoteca
Neighborhood wine bar with an Italian accent offers a range of small dishes for sharing along with 60 wines by the glass. ◈ 26 Charles St • Map M2 • 617 723 5939 • $$$$

3 Lala Rokh
Authentic Persian cuisine is served in this casual spot. Citrus-based glazes and relishes give meats amazing piquant flavor. ◈ 97 Mount Vernon St • Map N3 • 617 720 5511 • Closed lunch Sat & Sun • $$$

4 Artù
Tuscan specialties like lamb sandwiches and roasted veggies come sizzling off the grill on to the table. ◈ 89 Charles St • Map M3 • 617 227 9023 • Closed lunch Sun & Mon • $$$

5 Figs
This popular spot created by local celeb-chef Todd English specializes in pizza with toppings like artichoke, caramelized leeks, goat's cheese, and basil oil. ◈ 42 Charles St • Map M3 • 617 742 3447 • Closed lunch Mon–Fri • $$

6 Beacon Hill Bistro
This kitchen (in the Beacon Hill Hotel) puts an American stamp on French bistro cuisine to great effect. ◈ 25 Charles St • Map M3 • 617 723 1133 • Open for brunch Sat & Sun, closed lunch Sat & Sun • $$$$

7 Scampo
Bold design and Italian cuisine with a twist graces the first floor of the swank Liberty Hotel. ◈ Liberty Hotel, 215 Charles St • Map F3 • 617 536 2100 • $$$

8 Seven's Ale House
The epitome of a local Boston bar: dark wood, slightly surly staff, amiable patrons, a dartboard, and a rudimentary pub menu. ◈ 77 Charles St • Map M3

9 75 Chestnut
This converted townhouse offers one of Beacon Hill's most refined, romantic dining experiences. The menu offers affordable American bistro dishes. ◈ 75 Chestnut St • Map M3 • 617 227 2175 • Closed lunch except Sat & Sun brunch • $$$

10 21st Amendment
This neighborhood pub near the State House is a classy spot for legislators and movers and shakers to indulge in a tipple or two. ◈ 150 Bowdoin St • Map G3

Note: Reservations are recommended for most Beacon Hill restaurants

Left **Berklee Performance Center** Center **Portico, Trinity Church** Right **Café, Newbury Street**

Back Bay

THE EASILY NAVIGATED GRID OF STREETS *in Back Bay bears little resemblance to the labyrinthine lanes around Downtown and the North End. In the mid-1800s Back Bay was filled in to accommodate Boston's mushrooming population and by the late 1800s, the area had become a vibrant, upscale neighborhood. Home to many of Boston's wealthiest families, the area was characterized by lavish houses, grand churches, and bustling commercial zones. Many of the original buildings stand intact, providing an exquisite 19th-century backdrop for today's pulsing nightlife, world-class shopping, and sumptuous dining.*

Prudential Center

TOP 10 Attractions

1. Newbury Street
2. Trinity Church
3. Boston Public Library
4. The Esplanade
5. Berklee Performance Center
6. Commonwealth Avenue
7. Prudential Center
8. Christian Science Center
9. Gibson House Museum
10. New England Life Murals

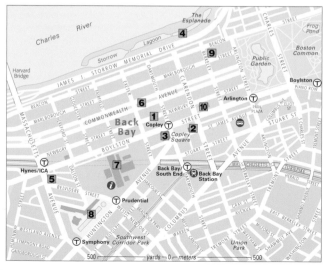

Note: *Cross streets in Back Bay run alphabetically, beginning with Arlington in the east and ending at Hereford Street in the west*

1 Newbury Street
Over the years, Back Bay's most famous street has proven to be amazingly adaptable. How else could fashion boutiques as *au courant* as Diesel and DKNY blend so seamlessly into their mid-19th-century brownstone environs? This uncanny adaptability provides for the liveliest, most eclectic street scene in Boston: a babble of languages, skater punks walking alongside catwalk models, and delivery trucks and Ferraris jockeying for the same parking space – it's all here (see pp20–21).

2 Trinity Church
When I. M. Pei's 60-story John Hancock Tower was completed in 1976, Bostonians feared Trinity Church would be overshadowed by its gleaming upstart neighbor. Yet H. H. Richardson's masterpiece, dedicated in 1877, remains just as vital to Copley Square, and as beautiful, as it appeared on its opening day (see pp26–7).

3 Boston Public Library
Although this McKim, Mead, and White-designed building went up in 1895, the Boston Public

Sargent mural, Boston Public Library

The Esplanade

Library was actually founded in 1848 and is the oldest publicly funded library in the country. The interior's Greco-Roman style cues lavish use of marble, and John Singer Sargent's powerful "Judaism and Christianity" mural sequence clearly illustrates how valued public education was when the library was constructed. Guided tours offer insight into the building's architecture and history.
⚅ 700 Boylston St • Map L5 • 617 536 5400 • Open 9am–9pm Mon–Thu, 9am–5pm Fri & Sat, 1–5pm Sun (Jun–Sep. closed Sun) • Tours: 2:30pm Mon, 6pm Tue & Thu, 11am Wed, Fri & Sat, 2pm Sun • Free • www.bpl.org

4 The Esplanade
The perfect setting for a leisurely bike ride, an invigorating jog, or a lazy afternoon of soaking up the sun, the Esplanade is one of the city's most popular green spaces. This ribbon of green hugging the Charles' river banks was inspired by Venetian canals. July 4th (see p54) at the Esplanade's Hatch Shell concert venue brings the world-famous Boston Pops orchestra along with thousands of revelers to enjoy the incomparable mix of music, good cheer, and awe-inspiring fireworks. Best avoided late at night. ⚅ Map M3

Bates Hall, Boston Public Library

For information on the origins of Back Bay See pp20–21
For information on Boston Common See pp14–15

5 Berklee Performance Center

The largest independent music school in the world, Berklee was founded in 1945. The college has produced a number of world-renowned jazz, rock, and pop stars, including Quincy Jones, Melissa Etheridge, Kevin Eubanks, Jan Hammer, and Branford Marsalis.

Mapparium, Christian Science Center

The state-of-the-art performance center hosts special events including concerts, plays, and film screenings.

§ *136 Massachusetts Ave • Map J6 • 617 266 7455 • Check website for details of concerts and performances: www.berkleebpc.com*

6 Commonwealth Avenue

With its leafy pedestrian mall and *belle époque*-inspired architecture, Commonwealth Avenue aptly deserves its comparison to *les rues parisiennes*. A morning jog on the mall is a popular pastime, as is the occasional picnic or afternoon snooze on a bench. Highlights include Boston's First Baptist Church (110 Clarendon; closed to non-worshipers) and the pedestrian mall's stately statues, including the William Lloyd Garrison bronze, sculpted by local artist Anne Whitney. § *Map J5–L4*

Baptist Church window, Commonwealth Ave

7 Prudential Center

Although difficult to imagine, the Prudential Tower's 52 stories seem dwarfed by the huge swathe of street-level shops and restaurants that comprise the Prudential Center. With its indoor shopping mall, food court, supermarket, cluster of residential towers, and massive convention center, the Prudential Center is like a self-contained city within a city. For a jaw-dropping view of Boston, visit the Skywalk on the tower's 50th level *(see p61)*, or the Top of the Hub Lounge *(see p88)* two floors above. § *800 Boylston St • Map K6 • 617 236 3100 • Open 10am–9pm Mon–Sat, 11am–6pm Sun*

8 Christian Science Center

While believers head for the Romanesque-Byzantine basilica, the library (entered from Massachusetts Avenue) emphasizes inspirational facets of the founder's life rather than church doctrine. The Mapparium, a walk-through stained-glass globe with 1935 political boundaries, remains the most popular exhibit. Peer into the newsroom of the Christian Science Monitor. Outside, a 670 ft- (204-m-) long reflecting pool designed by I. M. Pei is lined with begonias, marigolds, and columbines. The café is a good spot for lunch. § *175 Huntington Ave • Map K6 • 617 450 7000 • Library open 10am–4pm Tue–Sun • Adm • www.marybakereddylibrary.org*

Note: *For those tight on time, the Prudential Center's glorified food hall makes perfect sense*

Gibson House Museum

One of the first private residences to be built in Back Bay (c.1859), Gibson House remains beautifully intact. The house has been preserved as a monument to the era, thanks largely to the efforts of its final resident (the grandson of the well-to-do woman who built the house). So frozen in time does this house appear that you might feel like you're intruding on someone's inner sanctum, and an earlier age. Highlights of the tour include some elegant porcelain dinnerware, 18th-century heirloom jewelry, and exquisite black walnut woodwork throughout the house. ◈ 137 Beacon St • Map M4 • 617 267 6338 • Tours 1pm, 2pm & 3pm Wed–Sun • Adm • www.thegibsonhouse.org

Library, Gibson House Museum

New England Life Murals

In the lobby of this landmark 1939 building, a series of eight murals depicts scenes from Boston's most formative moments. Mounted in 1942 by a Beaux Arts star pupil, Charles Hoffbauer, the series commemorates events such as the pilgrims' welcome by the Samoset Indians in 1621 and the 1797 launching of the USS Constitution (see p30). ◈ 501 Boylston St • Map M5 • Open 9am–5pm Mon–Sat • Free

Exploring Back Bay

Afternoon

🕐 Grab a patio table at the **Parish Café** (see p45) and enjoy an inventive sandwich while gazing out onto the **Public Garden**. Stroll one block over to Newbury Street and peruse the impressive contemporary art galleries concentrated between Arlington and Dartmouth streets. Cross back over to Boylston at Dartmouth and sit for a spell inside **Trinity Church** (see pp26–7) where La Farge's stained-glass windows top an inexhaustible list of highlights. And while you're in an aesthetics-appreciating mood, traverse St James Place to the **Copley Plaza Hotel** and lounge a moment in the ornate, Versailles-esque lobby. Next, cross Dartmouth to the **Boston Public Library** (see p81) and admire John Singer Sargent's gorgeous murals. Now it's time to warm up your credit card, so head back to Newbury Street for a dizzying shopping spree. Turn left onto Newbury for Boston-only boutiques such as **Fresh** (see p85) and **Trident Booksellers** (see p85). Stop for a reinvigorating fruit smoothie or thick frappé at **Ben & Jerry's** (174 Newbury St). At Massachusetts Avenue, turn left, then left again onto Boylston and continue to the **Prudential Center** for name-brand shopping – think Saks Fifth Avenue, Neiman Marcus, and the like. Cap it all off with a bracing-cold cocktail and smooth jazz at the 52nd-floor **Top of the Hub Lounge** (see p88), where you can soak in Boston's skyline – and, with any luck, a dazzling sunset.

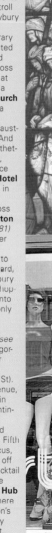

Left **Detail of work by John Walker, Neilsen** Right **Work by Sol Lewitt, Barbara Krakow Gallery**

Art Galleries

1 Robert Klein
Everybody who's anybody in photography vies for space at Robert Klein. Past coups include shows by Annie Leibovitz and Herb Ritts. *38 Newbury St • Map M5 • 617 267 7997 • Closed Sun & Mon*

2 Copley Society of Art
With a commitment to exhibiting works by promising New England artists, this non-profit organization has been providing young artists with that crucial first break since 1879. *158 Newbury St • Map L5 • 617 536 5049 • Closed Mon*

3 Gallery NAGA
Representing some of New England's most regarded artists, NAGA is possibly Newbury's best contemporary art gallery. *67 Newbury St • Map M5 • 617 267 9060 • Closed Sun & Mon*

4 Barbara Krakow Gallery
Since opening in 1964 with an exhibition of Ellsworth Kelly prints, Barbara Krakow's keen judgment of contemporary art has earned her many fans – and customers. *10 Newbury St • Map M5 • 617 262 4490 • Closed Sun & Mon*

5 Arden Gallery
This contemporary art gallery focuses on original paintings and sculpture, including bronze and other metals. It showcases up-and-coming abstract and realist artists. *129 Newbury St • Map L5 • 617 247 0610 • Closed Sun*

6 Society of Arts & Crafts
Devoted to art in craft media, this 1897 pioneer of artisanship, sells a wide variety of studio crafts. Jewelry and ceramics also available. *175 Newbury St • Map L5 • 617 266 1810 • Closed Sun & Mon*

7 Vose Galleries
The oldest family-owned art gallery in the US (open since 1841), Vose specializes in American realist painting and works on paper from the 18th–20th centuries. *238 Newbury St • Map K5 • 617 536 6176 • Closed Sun & Mon*

8 Alpha Gallery
Founded in 1967 to showcase contemporary artists from Boston, Alpha now covers the country and carries an impressive line of prints by modern masters. *37 Newbury St • Map M5 • 617 536 4465 • Closed Sun & Mon*

9 Neilsen Gallery
Favoring lush, contemporary paintings, and the occasional mixed-media sculpture, Neilsen is popular among Boston's art cognoscenti. *179 Newbury St • Map L5 • 978 369 7071 • Open by appointment only*

10 International Poster Gallery
Arguably the most fun – albeit the most populist – gallery on Newbury, the IPG stocks vintage first-edition movie posters and print advertisements from the belle époque. *205 Newbury St • Map K5 • 617 375 0076*

Note: *Unless otherwise specified galleries are open daily. Opening hours are generally from 10am–5:30pm*

Left **Trident Booksellers & Café** Right **Newbury Comics**

🔟 Homegrown Newbury Shops

1 Johnny Cupcakes
This boutique specializes in limited-edition crossbones-and-cupcake T-shirts. The joke continues with bakery case displays, aprons on the staff, and the smell of cake batter in the air.
◈ *279 Newbury St • Map K6*

2 Trident Booksellers & Café
Trident is popular for its delicious, healthy sandwiches, strong coffee concoctions, and arguably the best informed book and magazine selections in the city. ◈ *338 Newbury St • Map K6*

3 Hempest
True believers in the superiority of hemp as something to put on rather than inhale, Hempest showcases casual and dress duds fashioned from this environmentally friendly fiber.
◈ *207 Newbury St • Map K5*

4 Fresh
Chic grooming products for men and women, many of them based on such natural products as sugar (for face and body skin polish), clay (masks and lotions), and soy (facial cleaning gel).
◈ *121 Newbury St • Map L5*

5 Newbury Comics
Generally undercutting the chain stores on compact discs, Newbury Comics delivers value along with a stellar selection of rare import CDs, concert videos, and the latest comics. ◈ *332 Newbury St • Map J6*

6 Life is Good
This feel-good store name has swept through America. The collection offers youth fashion with whimsical images emblazoned on casual clothes.
◈ *285 Newbury St • Map K5*

7 Second Time Around
Before blowing your budget on that Chanel handbag, take a peek at Second Time Around, where used designer clothing and accessories get a second lease on life. Think head-to-toe Versace for a mere $100. ◈ *176 Newbury St • Map L5*

8 Condom World
Check your inhibitions at this subterranean boutique's door. While male anatomy shaped ketchup dispensers deserve a laugh, some of the sex toys toward the back might sooner merit a wince. ◈ *332 Newbury St • Map J6*

9 Simon Pearce
Fine blown glass and hand-made pottery from eponymous Irish designer and artist creates tableware with an upscale touch. Pearce signatures include classic goblets and other stemware.
◈ *103 Newbury St • Map F4*

10 Deluca's Back Bay Market
This old world-style corner market stocks fabulous produce, chilled beer, ready-made sandwiches, and imported delights of all kinds. ◈ *239 Newbury St • Map K5*

➤ **Note:** *Unless otherwise specified shops are open daily*

Left Akris Right Teuscher Chocolates of Switzerland

TOP 10 Shops to Drain your Bank Account

1 Diane von Furstenberg
Feminine elegance for women of all sizes is DVF's signature, and it's abundant at her Boston boutique. Look for super cocktail dresses and sophisticated details such as leather trim. ⬡ 74 Newbury St • Map F4

2 Shreve, Crump & Low
The country's oldest retail jeweler has seen its diamonds grace the fingers of some of modern history's most famous – and fortunate – figures. Shreve's sterling silver is also highly coveted. ⬡ 39 Newbury St • Map M5

3 Alan Bilzerian
From a $4,000 John Galliano silk dress to a skimpy camouflage Christian Dior bikini, Alan Bilzerian is the place to go for high-end fashion that exudes personality. ⬡ 34 Newbury St • Map M5 • Closed Sun

4 Ermenegildo Zegna
For the successful businessman whose daydreams feature a vintage Ferrari and the Sardinian coast, Zegna fits like a glove. Classic Italian suits and ties that are unrivaled for style and quality. ⬡ 100 Huntington Ave #19 • Map M5

5 Burberry
Helpful sales staff make shopping in this outpost of British style a pleasure. Prices may be high (watch out for sales), but classic design makes each trench coat or bag a long-term investment. ⬡ 2 Newbury St • Map M5

6 Bang & Olufsen
Who said entertainment technology must look tacky? Danish postmodern design creates music systems, televisions, telephones, and even remote controls with a great deal of style. ⬡ 141B Newbury St • Map F4

7 Lux, Bond & Green
While not quite as prestigious as its neighbor Shreve, Green still manages with Tag Heuer watches, Mikimoto pearls, and Garavelli diamonds at prices that remain this side of the stratosphere. ⬡ 416 Boylston St • Map M5 • Closed Sun

8 Converse Shop
The famed maker of sneakers for basketball stars and rock musicians started in Boston, so it was only fitting that the first Converse retail shop should open here too. ⬡ 348 Newbury St • Map E5 • 617 424 5400

9 Akris
Footware by Jimmy Choo and Stuart Wietzman claim the back of the store, while cashmere suits, evening gowns, and luxurious coats rule the racks up front. ⬡ 16 Newbury St • Map M5 • Closed Sun

10 Teuscher Chocolates of Switzerland
Relishing a Teuscher truffle ranks among life's greatest pleasures. Perhaps no other chocolatier in the world gets the alchemy quite so right. ⬡ 230 Newbury St • Map K5

Note: Unless otherwise specified shops are open daily

Price Categories

For a three course meal for one with half a bottle of wine (or equivalent meal), taxes, and extra charges.	**$** under $30
	$$ $30–$45
	$$$ $45–$60
	$$$$ $60–$75
	$$$$$ over $75

Above **Sidewalk dining**

Alfresco Scenes

Salty Pig
Start with porcine charcuterie (from speck to pig tails), add a stinky cheese, then some fig jam, and you have a dish typical of Salty Pig. Alternatively, opt for pizza or pasta at a sidewalk table. ◎ *130 Dartmouth St • Map F5 • $*

Sonsie
With windows that open up on to the street, Sonsie sets the alfresco standard at this end of Newbury. The fashionable clientele enjoy light Italocentric cuisine upstairs, and devilish cocktails in the basement Red Room. ◎ *327 Newbury St • Map J6 • 617 351 2500 • $$*

Stephanie's on Newbury
Enjoying one of the most generous portions of Newbury sidewalk, this American bistro packs the tables for the likes of duck and porcini risotto. ◎ *190 Newbury St • Map L5 • 617 236 0990 • $$$$*

Tapéo
Experience a sultry Barcelona night: Newbury's most romantic alfresco nighttime scene combines intensely flavorful tapas and an extensive Spanish wine list. ◎ *266 Newbury St • Map K5 • 617 267 4799 • Closed lunch Mon–Fri • $$$*

Ciao Bella
Ciao Bella is a favorite stop for star athletes, who come for the hearty portions of no-frills Italian cuisine and the sizzling alfresco scene. ◎ *240 Newbury St • Map K5 • 617 536 2626 • $$$*

Davio's
With a versatile menu of robust Italian specialties, design-your-own pizzas, and a spacious sidewalk café, Davio's is sure to please. ◎ *75 Arlington St • Map M5 • 617 357 4810 • $$$$*

Joe's American Bar & Grill
Although the white tablecloths might suggest refined dining, Joe's fits squarely in the glorified-burger milieu. Its patio boasts prime people-watching and the staff are kid-friendly. ◎ *181 Newbury St • Map L5 • 617 536 4200 • $$$*

Parish Café
This split-level café with a patio has a lovely view onto the Public Garden (see pp14–15) and an inspired menu of delicious and wildly creative sandwiches. ◎ *361 Boylston St • Map M5 • $$*

L'Aroma
Casual and calorie-conscious food along with high-octane espresso make sure that upscale Newbury Street shoppers can survive to the next boutique. ◎ *85 Newbury St • Map L5 • $*

Bistro du Midi
Savor great versions of classic dishes such as seared foie gras and hearty Provençal beef daube at this French bistro with North African accents. Sidewalk tables offer a view of the Public Garden. ◎ *272 Boylston St • Map F4 • $$$*

Left **29 Newbury** Right **Top of the Hub Lounge**

🔟 Nightclubs & Bars

1 Top of the Hub Lounge
Talk about a view: 52 stories above Back Bay, this bar dazzles with sweeping views, live jazz, and a wicked gin martini.
⊗ *Prudential Tower, 800 Boylston St • Map K6 • Closes 1am Sun–Wed*

2 Daisy Buchanan's
Professional athletes, models, and local professionals are drawn to Daisy's for its friendly, casual vibe. ⊗ *240 Newbury St • Map K5*

3 Kings
The fifties were never so cool as they seem at this retro-styled lounge, pool hall, and bowling alley buried downstairs next to the Hynes Convention Center. ⊗ *10 Scotia St • Map J6*

4 Storyville
Speakeasy meets nightclub at this lounge which serves hip bar food such as short rib casserole, and snazzy cocktails. ⊗ *94 Exeter St • Map F5 • Closed Sun–Tue*

5 Whiskey's
Be sure to have ID in hand before putting pint to mouth at this lively bar. It's full of hard-drinking collegiate types, who arrive around 6pm and stay until last call. ⊗ *885 Boylston St • Map K6*

6 Bar at the Taj
Boston's elite have been meeting and socializing at this elegant room facing the Public Garden since the 1920s. ⊗ *15 Arlington St • Map F4 • Closes 11:30pm*

7 The Pour House
Cheap, hearty pub grub and occasional drink specials lure college kids to this two-story bar and grill. It's loud, it's crowded, and you're bound to make a friend or two. ⊗ *907 Boylston St • Map K6*

8 Bukowski Tavern
A beer drinker's paradise, Bukowski counts 100 varieties of suds. Its primary patrons are a professional crowd during the day and young hipsters at night.
⊗ *50 Dalton St • Map K6*

9 29 Newbury
With a rotating art gallery and excellent contemporary dining room, 29 Newbury's bar draws a well-heeled, mature crowd that enjoys the serious cocktails. ⊗ *29 Newbury St • Map M5 • Closes 1am*

10 Cactus Club
Some bars have martini menus, but at the Cactus Club it's all about the margarita, with a nod to tequilas, straight up or with a rim of salt. Very sociable singles scene. ⊗ *939 Boylston St • Map J6*

> **Note:** *Unless otherwise specified, bars and nightclubs are open until 2am daily*

Price Categories

For a three course meal for one with half a bottle of wine (or equivalent meal), taxes, and extra charges.	**$** under $30
	$$ $30–$45
	$$$ $45–$60
	$$$$ $60–$75
	$$$$$ over $75

Left **Sorellina**

🔟 Restaurants

1 Sorellina
Regional Italian food with a contemporary spin is accompanied by great wines and served up in a sophisticated dining room. ◈ *1 Huntingdon Ave • Map F5 • 617 412 4600 • $$$$*

2 L'Espalier
New England ingredients combine with high-style modern French technique to create memorable, luxury dining. ◈ *774 Boylston St • Map K6 • 617 262 3023 • $$$$$*

3 Deuxave
Elegant contemporary dining ranges from local lobster and scallops to caramelized onion ravioli ◈ *371 Commonwealth Ave • Map E5 • 617 517 5915 • Closed lunch • $$$$$*

4 Grill 23
Grill 23 harkens back to the days of exclusive, Prohibition-era supper clubs. Prime aged beef with an inventive spin is served in a sumptuously classic interior. ◈ *161 Berkeley St • Map M5 • 617 542 2255 • Closed lunch • $$$$$*

5 Post 390
This urban tavern near the South End border is a comfortable meeting spot, with three fireplaces, two bars, and an open kitchen on two levels. ◈ *406 Stuart St • Map M5 • 617 399 0015 • Closed lunch Sat & Sun • $$$$*

6 Clio
Chef Ken Oringer presides over the grand Eliot Hotel's claim to culinary fame. Luxurious entrées complement the richly appointed dining room. ◈ *370A Commonwealth Ave • Map J5 • 617 536 7200 • Closed lunch & Mon • $$$$$*

7 Via Matta
"Crazy Street" is an apt name for the lively bar scene that accompanies top northern Italian cuisine. ◈ *79 Park Plaza • Map M5 • 617 422 0008 • $$$$*

8 Brasserie Jo
Bustling Brasserie Jo captures the *savoir faire* of 1940s Paris. Hearty French classics like steak roquefort. ◈ *120 Huntington Ave • Map K6 • 617 425 3240 • $$$*

9 Erbaluce
Chef Charles Draghi brings French technical finesse to north Italian cuisine with a menu that changes nightly. ◈ *60 Church St • Map G5 • 617 426 6969 • $$$*

10 Douzo
The serene setting makes the city's best sushi restaurant something of a Zen experience. ◈ *131 Dartmouth St • Map L6 • 617 859 8886 • $$$$*

Note: *Unless otherwise specified, restaurants are open for lunch and dinner daily. Reservations are generally required*

89

Left **Copp's Hill Burying Ground** Right **New England Aquarium**

North End & the Waterfront

THE NORTH END IS BOSTON'S ITALIAN VILLAGE, *where feast day blends into feast day all summer as the great-grandchildren of Southern Italian immigrants celebrate the music, food, and dolce vita of the old country. Every other storefront houses a restaurant, café, or bakery and the cheers of European football fans echo from the bars. These transplanted festivities continue year round, merely moving indoors when the season chills. Yet the North End predates its Italian inhabitants and the neighborhood is in fact the oldest in Boston. The perimeter of the area along the waterfront bristles with condo developments on the former shipping piers, which lead south to the bustle of Long, Central, and Rowes wharves. Boston was born by the sea and it is now reclaiming its waterfront as a vital center for business and pleasure.*

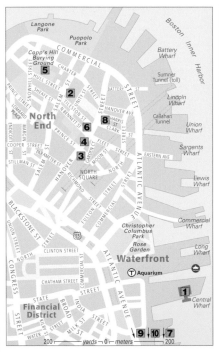

Old North Church

🔟 Attractions

1. New England Aquarium
2. Old North Church
3. Paul Revere House
4. Hanover Street
5. Copp's Hill Burying Ground
6. Paul Revere Mall
7. Institute of Contemporary Art
8. St. Stephen's Church
9. Children's Museum
10. Boston Tea Party Ships & Museum

Note: *The Freedom Trail (see pp8–9) passes the Paul Revere House, Old North Church, and Copp's Hill Burying Ground*

1 New England Aquarium

Now the centerpiece of the downtown waterfront development, the aquarium's construction in the 1960s paved the way for the revitalization of Boston Harbor. Seals cavort in a tank in front of the sleek modern structure (see p32–3). ✪ Map R3

2 Old North Church

An active Episcopal congregation still worships at Boston's oldest church, officially known as Christ Church (1723). The austere interior looks much as it did in its early days. It was here, in 1775, that sexton Robert Newman hung two lanterns in the belfry to warn horseback messenger Paul Revere of British troop movements (see p10). ✪ 193 Salem St • Map Q1 • 617 523 6676 • Open Jun–Oct: 9am–6pm daily (shorter hours off-season) • Donation • www.oldnorth.com

Hanover Street

Old North Church clock

3 Paul Revere House

Home to Paul Revere for 30 years, this 17th-century clapboard house is the only surviving home of any of Boston's revolutionary heroes. It provides an intriguing glimpse into the domestic life of Revere's family with displays of their furniture and possessions including silverwork

Paul Revere House

made by Revere, who was highly regarded as a metalsmith. Well-trained staff narrate the tale of Revere's legendary midnight ride (see p10). ✪ 19 North Sq • Map Q1 • 617 523 2338 • Open mid-Apr–Oct: 9:30am–5:15pm daily; Nov–mid Apr: 9:30am–4:15pm daily (closed Mon Jan–Mar) • Adm • limited DA • www.paulreverehouse.org

4 Hanover Street

Originally built in the 17th-century to connect the shipping wharves to Dock Square (now Faneuil Hall Marketplace; see pp12–13), Hanover Street was widened in 1870 to accommodate the busy flow of commerce. Today, as the North End's principal artery with cafés and eateries aplenty, it is the place to come for a slice of the action. ✪ Map Q2

5 Copp's Hill Burying Ground

Trace the history of Boston on the thousands of tombstones here, from the mean-spirited Mather family, theocrats who ruled the early city, to the valiant patriots slain in the fight for freedom. In the Battle of Bunker Hill (see p10), the British, who occupied the city in 1775, manned a battery from this site and fired on neighboring Charlestown. There are sweeping views of the harbor. ✪ Entrance on Hull St • Map Q1 • Open 9am–5pm daily • No DA • 617 635 4505

 Note: Feast days of North End patron saints are celebrated with street parties and parades most weekends from mid-June through August

Foraging for Formaggio

Italian food, wine, and culture expert Michele Topor has lived in the North End for four decades. Her tour of the local markets on Wednesday and Saturday (10am, 1pm, 2pm, 5pm), and Friday (10am, 1pm, 3pm, 6pm) includes tastings and insights on local restaurants. To reserve a place, contact Boston Food Tours: 800 979 3370, www.bostonfoodtours.com.

Paul Revere Mall

The North End's history as both revolutionary stronghold and Italian immigrant neighborhood comes together along this tree-lined mall, which old-timers persist in calling the Prado. Created in 1933, the pedestrian mall connects Hanover Street to the rear of Old North Church. Bronze plaques lining the walls capture snippets from the lives of former Bostonians, while an equestrian statue of Paul Revere surveys it all. Today, the mall is a social center, where mothers convene with baby carriages, kids play frisbee, and old men hunker over checkerboards. Map Q1

Institute of Contemporary Art

The ICA was founded in 1936 and reopened in its modern

St. Stephen's Church

landmark structure on Fan Pier in 2006. The striking glass, wood, and steel building, designed by Diller Scofidio & Renfro, is cantilevered over the Harbor Walk and provides dramatic views. The ICA promotes cutting-edge art and focuses on 21st-century work. There is also a program of performing arts. *100 Northern Ave • 617 478 3100 • Open 10am–5pm Tue, Wed, Sat & Sun, 10am–9pm Thu & Fri • Adm • www.icaboston.org*

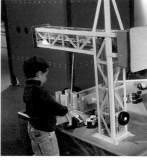

Children's Museum

St. Stephen's Church

Renowned architect Charles Bulfinch completely redesigned the church's original 1714 structure in 1802–4. This church is the only surviving example of his religious architecture. The complex Neo-Classical exterior contrasts with the open, airy, and relatively unadorned interior. In 1862, the Roman Catholic archdiocese took over the church to accomodate the area's growing number of Irish immigrants. Rose Fitzgerald, daughter of Boston mayor John "Honey Fitz" Fitzgerald and mother of President J. F. Kennedy *(see p39)*, is linked to the church. She was baptized here in 1890, and her funeral took place here in 1995. *401 Hanover St • Map R1 • 617 523 1230 • Open 8:30am–4:30pm Mon–Sat, 11am Sun for worship • Free*

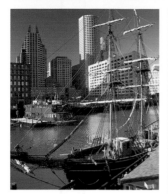

Boston Tea Party Ship

Children's Museum

Educators at this ground-breaking interactive museum for kids pioneered some of the features now found in similar facilities around the world, including giant soap bubbles and complex rampways for marbles (see p60).

Boston Tea Party Ships & Museum

The historic occasion known as the Boston Tea Party, when patriots dressed as native Americans and threw a consignment of English tea overboard to protest against the Stamp Tax of 1773, proved to be a precipitating event of the American Revolution (see p10). The Boston Tea Party ships are replicas of three vessels that were relieved of their cargo that fateful December night. Costumed storytellers recount events in rousing detail, and visitors can board one of the vessels and re-enact the destruction of the tea. In the museum is one of two tea crates known to have survived from the incident, while Abigail's Tea Room serves up a nice "cuppa". ◈ Congress St Bridge • Map R5 • 855 TEA 1773 • Open 9am–5pm daily • Adm • www.bostonteapartyship.com

From Narrow Byways to the Sea

Morning

🕐 From the Haymarket "T", follow Hanover Street to Richmond Street and continue to North Square. Stop at **Paul Revere House** (see p91) for a glimpse of the domestic life of the revolutionary hero. Return to Hanover for an espresso and some prime people-watching at lively **Caffè Vittoria** (see p44). Continue up Hanover and turn left through Paul Revere Mall to **Old North Church** (see p91). The bust of George Washington inside is reputedly the world's most accurate rendering of his distinctive face – compare the resemblance to a dollar bill. Then stroll up Hull Street past **Copp's Hill Burying Ground** (see p91) for a great vantage point of USS Constitution (see p30) before continuing to the waterfront. Grab a bench in **Puopolo Park** to watch a match of bocce, an Italian lawn bowling game. Walk south along Commercial Street and stop for an alfresco waterside lunch at **Joe's American Bar & Grill** (100 Atlantic Ave).

Afternoon

Resume your waterfront stroll along the Rose Kennedy Greenway and stop off to enjoy the roses in the **Rose Kennedy Rose Garden**, before whiling away an hour or so in the **New England Aquarium** (see pp32–3) where highlights include the swirling Giant Ocean Tank. Relax with a sun-downer on the patio of the **Boston Harbor Hotel** (70 Rowes Wharf) before you head to **Sel de la Terre** (see p95) for a Provençal dinner.

Note: Numerous water tours and excursions leave from Long Wharf including trips to the Boston Harbor Islands See pp66–7

Left **Monica's Mercato** Right **Polcari's Coffee Co.**

TOP 10 Italian Bakeries & Grocers

1 Mike's Pastry
Large glass cases display a huge selection of cookies and *cannoli* (crunchy pastry filled with a sweet ricotta cream). Purchase a box to go, or grab a table and order a drink and a delectable pastry. ⊗ *300 Hanover St • Map Q1*

2 Salumeria Italiana
This neighborhood fixture is a premier stop for esoteric Italian canned goods and rich olive oils, as well as spicy sausages and cheeses from many Italian regions. ⊗ *151 Richmond St • Map Q2 • Closed Sun • No DA*

3 Modern Pastry
House specialties here include rich ricotta pie and nougat made on the premises, as well as chocolate truffles from Italy and delicate Florentines. Modern makes a thinner *cannoli* shell than Mike's. ⊗ *257 Hanover St • Map Q2*

4 Polcari's Coffee Co.
The premier bulk grocer in the North End, this charming store has sold Italian roasted coffee since 1932. It's still the best place to find spices, flours, grains, and legumes. ⊗ *105 Salem St • Map Q1 • Closed Sun • No DA*

5 Bova's Bakery
Fresh bread emerges from the ovens at all hours. When the bars and coffee shops close, night owls head to Bova's for hot sandwiches and cookies. ⊗ *134 Salem St • Map Q1 • No DA*

6 V. Cirace Wine & Spirits
The North End's most upscale seller of Italian wines and liqueurs stocks both fine wines to lay down and cheerfully youthful ones to enjoy right away. ⊗ *173 North St • Map Q2 • Closed Sun • No DA*

7 Monica's Mercato
Linked to a nearby restaurant, this *salumeria* has the usual cheeses and sausages, but its specialties are prepared foods such as cold salads for picnics and pasta dishes for reheating. ⊗ *130 Salem St • Map Q1 • No DA*

8 Maria's Pastry Shop
Run for three generations by the Merola family, Maria's is famed for its Neapolitan flaky and sweet *sfogliatelle* (filled pastry) as well as its seasonal sweets, such as chocolate-allspice cookies at Christmas and marzipan lambs at Easter. ⊗ *46 Cross St • Map Q2 • Closed Sun*

9 The Cheese Shop
This shop serves fresh ricotta and mozzarella with rare, imported Italian cheeses. ⊗ *20 Fleet St • Map R1*

10 DePasquale's Homemade Pasta Shoppe
With some 50 varieties of fresh pasta made daily, plus sauces, pesto, grating cheeses, and a handful of hard-to-find Italian groceries, DePasquale's is one-stop shopping. Ask for sauce pairings. ⊗ *66A Cross St • Map H13*

Note: *Unless otherwise specified, all bakeries and grocers are open daily*

Left **Maurizio's**

⑩ Restaurants & Bars

Price Categories

For a three course meal for one with half a bottle of wine (or equivalent meal), taxes, and extra charges.	**$** under $30
	$$ $30–$45
	$$$ $45–$60
	$$$$ $60–$75
	$$$$$ over $75

Maurizio's
A cozy, buzzy spot where chef Maurizio Lodo draws on his Sardinian heritage to create dishes that often include brilliant preparations of fish. ❧ *364 Hanover St • Map Q1 • 617 367 1123 • Closed Mon • No DA • $$$*

Taranta
An artistic blend of Sardinian and Peruvian cuisine spells intense flavors (pork with vinegar peppers and broccoli). ❧ *210 Hanover St • Map Q2 • 617 720 0052 • Closed lunch Sun • No DA • $$$$*

Legal Harborside
The flagship of the Legal Sea Foods chain offers fish lovers three floors of seafood heaven. Book ahead for fine dining on level two *(see p42)*.

Aragosta
Stunning waterfront views complement Mediterranean flavors and New England seafood at the Fairmont Hotel ❧ *3 Battery Wharf • Map H2 • 617 994 9001 • Closed dinner Sun • $$$$*

Pizzeria Regina
The original Regina's thin crust, old-fashioned pizza is far better than the pale imitations served at its other branches. ❧ *11½ Thacher St • Map Q1 • No DA • $*

Sportello
Barbara Lynch's upscale lunch counter puts an Italian spin on comfort food with dishes like Roman gnocchi. ❧ *348 Congress St • Map I4 • 617 737 1234 • $$$*

Neptune Oyster
The delicate raw bar oysters are almost upstaged by large and bold roasted fish and pasta dishes in this tiny, stylish spot. Tables turn over quickly. ❧ *63 Salem St • Map Q1 • 617 742 3474 • $$$*

Ristorante Fiore
Traditional southern Italian cuisine with a strong Italian-American accent has made this a popular dining spot, especially with its outdoor rooftop terrace. ❧ *250 Hanover St • Map H1 • 617 371 1176 • Closed lunch Sun • $$$*

Sel de la Terre
Sunny tastes of Provence – down to homemade tapenade and hearth breads – make this a must for gourmets at lunch and dinner. ❧ *255 State St • Map R2 • 617 720 1300 • $$$$*

Prezza
One of the longest wine lists in town guarantees just the right glass to accompany hearty Tuscan fare as well as sinfully rich desserts. ❧ *24 Fleet St • Map R1 • 617 227 1577 • Closed lunch, Sun • $$$$*

Note: *Many restaurants in this area do not accept reservations (phone numbers have been given for those that do)*

Left **Post Office Square** Right **Interior, Quincy Market**

Downtown & the Financial District

THE HEART OF BOSTON *is sandwiched between Boston Common and the harbor. Unlike many US cities, Boston has great respect for its past and there are reminders of nearly four centuries of history embedded in the center of this modern metropolis. The 18th-century grace of historic buildings like the Old State House still shines within a canyon of skyscrapers. Even the heroes of Boston's early years remain here – city founder John Winthrop, patriot Paul Revere, and revolutionary Samuel Adams are buried just steps from sidewalks abuzz with shoppers. Rolled in to this amorphous area is Faneuil Hall Marketplace (see pp12–13), the oldest of Boston's commercial districts, and the Financial District, which stands as testament to Boston's continuing worldwide economic clout.*

Left **Downtown Crossing department store** Right **Financial District skyscrapers**

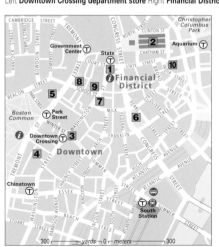

Attractions

1. Old State House
2. Faneuil Hall Marketplace
3. Downtown Crossing
4. Ladder District
5. Old Granary Burying Ground
6. Post Office Square
7. Old South Meeting House
8. King's Chapel
9. Old Corner Bookstore
10. Custom House

Sign up for DK's email newsletter on traveldk.com

1 Old State House

Built in 1713 as the seat of colonial government, the Old State House was designed to look down State Street to the shipping hub of Long Wharf. In 1770, the Boston Massacre *(see p10)* occurred outside its doors, and on July 18, 1776, the Declaration of Independence was first read to Bostonians from its balcony *(see p9)*. Today, it's home to the Bostonian Society & Old State House Museum. Ⓢ *Washington & State Sts • Map Q3 • 617 720 1713 • Open 9am–5pm daily (Jan: until 4pm; Jul–Aug: until 6pm) • Adm*

Central staircase, Old State House

2 Faneuil Hall Marketplace

Many a fiery speech urging revolution echoed in Faneuil Hall in the late 18th century; in the 1820s it was the city's food distribution that was revolutionized in adjacent Quincy Market. Today the buildings and surrounding plazas form a festival marketplace – the successful model for dozens of markets worldwide *(see pp12–13)*.

3 Downtown Crossing

This pedestrian-friendly shopping area is dominated by Macy's department store. Pushcart vendors offer more quirky goods, and food carts provide quick lunches for downtown office workers. Ⓢ *Junction of Summer, Winter & Washington Sts • Map P4*

4 Ladder District

The network of short streets

Vendor, Downtown Crossing

connecting Washington and Tremont streets has assumed a modern identity as the Ladder District. Once derelict and abandoned after dark, the area now throbs with clubs, bars, and restaurants. Anchoring the district, the Millennium Tower houses the ultra-chic Ritz-Carlton Boston Common *(see p146)* and the top-of-the-line Loews Cineplex (175 Tremont St). A few stalwarts, such as the landmark used-book seller, Brattle Book Shop, are holding out against the moneyed big boys. Ⓢ *Map P4*

5 Old Granary Burying Ground

Dating from 1660, the Granary contains the graves of many of Boston's most illustrious figures, including John Hancock, Samuel Adams, and Paul Revere *(see p38)*, who joined his revolutionary comrades here in 1818. Other notables include the hugely influential architect Charles Bulfinch, Benjamin Franklin's parents, and Crispus Attucks – an escaped slave who was allegedly the first casualty of the so-dubbed Boston Massacre *(see p10)*. Ⓢ *Tremont St at Park St • Map P3 • 617 635 4505 • Open 9am–5pm daily • Free*

Murals, New England Telephone building, Post Office Square

Post Office Square

On a sunny day this green oasis in the heart of the Financial District is filled with office workers who claim a bench or a spot of grass for a picnic. Surrounding the park are several of the area's most architecturally distinctive buildings, including the Art Deco post office building (Congress St), the Renaissance revival former Federal Reserve building (now the Langham Boston hotel, *see p146*), and the Art Moderne New England Telephone building (185 Franklin St). ◈ *Map Q3*

Old South Meeting House

Old South's rafters have rung with many impassioned speeches exhorting the overthrow of the king, the abolition of slavery,

Old South Meeting House

women's right to vote, an end to apartheid, and many other causes. Nearly abandoned when its congregation moved to Back Bay in 1876, it was saved in one of Boston's first acts of preservation. ◈ *310 Washington St • Map Q3 • 617 482 6439 • Open Apr–Oct: 9.30am– 5pm daily; Nov–Mar: 10am–4pm daily • Adm • www.oldsouthmeetinghouse.org*

Interior, King's Chapel

King's Chapel

The first Anglican Church in Puritan Boston was established in 1686 to serve the British Army officers. When the majority of Anglicans fled Boston along with retreating British forces in the evacuation of 1776, the chapel became the first Unitarian Church in the New World. The church is known for its program of classical concerts. Inquire about tours of the crypt and belltower. ◈ *58 Tremont St • Map P3 • 617 523 1749 • Open 10am–4pm daily. Recitals: 12:15pm Tue. Tours: adm • www.kings-chapel.org*

Old Corner Bookstore

This enduring spot on the Freedom Trail remains one of the most tangible sites associated with the writers of the New England Renaissance of the last half of the 19th century. Both the *Atlantic Monthly* magazine and

Ticknor & Fields (publishers of Ralph Waldo Emerson and Henry David Thoreau) made this modest structure its headquarters during the mid- and late 19th century, when Boston was the literary, intellectual, and publishing center of the country. Saving the site from demolition in 1960 led to the formation of Historic Boston Incorporated. The building, however, is no longer connected to publishing. ◈ *1 School St • Map P3*

Custom House

When the Custom House was built in 1840, Boston was one of America's largest overseas shipping ports, and customs fees were the mainstay of the Federal budget. The Neo-Classical structure once sat on the waterfront, but now stands two blocks inland. The 16-story Custom House tower, added in 1913, was Boston's first skyscraper. Since the 1990s, peregrine falcons have nested in the clock tower under the watchful eyes of wildlife biologists. The lobby displays a few historical artifacts, and tours of the tower give sweeping views of the harbor and city skyline. ◈ *3 McKinley Sq • Map Q3 • 617 310 6300 • Tours 2pm daily • Adm*

Custom House Tower

A Shopping Spree

Morning

🕐 The "T" will deposit you at Downtown Crossings, where you can peruse the fashions and accessories of **Macy's** at leisure. Then proceed to check out **H&M** (350 Washington St) for the latest in Euro styles and **DSW Shoe Warehouse** (385 Washington St) for a great selection of fashion shoes at discount prices. Make a left up Bromfield St to peruse the fine writing implements and elegant stationery at **Bromfield Pen Shop** (5 Bromfield St). The walk to Quincy Market down Franklin Street takes you past the Financial District with its tall and imposing skyscrapers. Turn left at Post Office Square for lunch at **Sip Café** (Post Office Square Park).

Afternoon

Stop to enjoy a short rest outside **Quincy Market** *(see p12)* before you begin your spree in earnest. Numerous name-brand shops such as **Victoria's Secret** await. For a more local flavor try the **Bill Rodgers Running Center** (North Market), which is operated by the champion Boston marathon runner. Then pay a visit to **Local Collection** for clothing and jewelry by local designers. Have an early dinner and make new friends at the communal tables at **Durgin-Park** (North Market, 617 227 2038). Order the gigantic prime rib and the Indian pudding (a cornmeal-molasses dish) for dessert. After dinner, rock out to live music at the **Hard Rock Café** (22–24 Clinton Street, 617 424 7625).

Following Pages **Custom House**

Left **Felt** Center **A pint of Guinness** Right **Bond Lounge**

🔟 Bars & Clubs

Good Life Downtown
This retro lounge lizard bar-restaurant jumps after work and on weekend nights with downtown execs. Cocktails are top notch. ⊗ *28 Kingston St • Map P4*

Mojito's
This vibrant Downtown Crossing nightspot has a lively, Latin music and dance scene on the weekends, and an enthusiastic international crowd. ⊗ *48 Winter St • Map P4*

Times Irish Pub & Bar
You can usually get a table at this large pub. Settle in for a night of live music and taste some of the 20 beers on tap. ⊗ *112 Broad St • Map R3*

Felt
With urban-chic style plus 14 pool tables, a club, and a restaurant spread over four floors, this is as smooth as it gets in the trendy Leather District. ⊗ *533 Washington St • Map P4*

Silvertone Bar & Grill
This surprisingly unpretentious, contemporary jazz bar and casual restaurant makes an excellent place to sip good value wine, kick back, and engage in intelligent conversation with your neighbors. ⊗ *69 Bromfield St • Map P3 • Closed Sun*

Parris
The strobe-lit hardwood nightclub floor beneath the Quincy Market rotunda is always heaving at this popular club. Don't miss the extensive martini menu. ⊗ *1 Faneuil Hall Market Pl • Map Q3*

Petite Robert Central
A quarter of this roomy bistro is devoted to the swank, Parisian-style bar, which has great cordials, wines, and cocktails. Try the classic Soixante Quinze. ⊗ *101 Arch St • Map G4*

Woodward at the Ames
A bold Modernist aesthetic rules the room, yet those oh-so-stylish chairs are both posh and comfy. Creative cocktails accompany the Scotch and Bourbons. ⊗ *Ames Hotel, 1 Court St • Map H3*

Bond Lounge
Easily the most exclusive watering hole in Boston, the Julien exudes old money, which is fitting for the former Governor's Reception Room of the Federal Reserve Bank. ⊗ *Langham Hotel, 250 Franklin St • Map Q3/4*

JM Curley
Named for Boston's old-time felonious mayor, this bar has good pub victuals (served until late) and an exhaustive list of craft and mass-market beers. ⊗ *21 Temple Pl • Map G4*

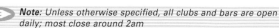

Note: *Unless otherwise specified, all clubs and bars are open daily; most close around 2am*

Price Categories

For a three course meal for one with half a bottle of wine (or equivalent meal), taxes, and extra charges.

$	under $30
$$	$30–$45
$$$	$45–$60
$$$$	$60–$75
$$$$$	over $75

Left **blu**

🔟 Restaurants for Luxury Dining

1 Bina Osteria
Imaginative but hearty fare from Sicily and southern Italy is complemented by the breezy contemporary decor. ◊ *3 Winter Pl • Map G4 • 617 956 0888 • Closed lunch Sat & Sun • $$$$*

2 Radius
Chef and co-owner Michael Schlow creates some of the most explosively sensual New American dishes in town.
◊ *8 High St • Map Q4 • 617 426 1234 • Closed lunch Sat, Sun • $$$$$*

3 blu
Light, fresh, delicately nuanced, and artistically presented international cuisine is complemented by soaring postmodern architecture. ◊ *4 Avery St • Map P4 • 617 375 8550 • $$$$*

4 KO Prime
A contemporary steakhouse in the Nine Zero hotel *(see p146)* with over-the-top cuts of prime meat, which are often basted with melted bone marrow. ◊ *90 Tremont St • Map P3 • 617 722 0202 • $$$$$*

5 Mantra
Indian flavors fused with French technique are found in this hip restaurant where the fine food makes up for the gimmicky decor.
◊ *52 Temple Pl • Map P4 • 617 542 8111 • Closed lunch Sat • $$$$$*

6 No 9 Park
Hobnob with Beacon Hill high flyers in this bold bistro overlooking Boston Common, where Mediterranean flavors meet an imaginative wine list. ◊ *9 Park St • Map P3 • 617 742 9991 • $$$$$*

7 Teatro
A glamourous hipster scene prevails at superchef Jamie Mammano's flashy trattoria, which boasts a killer wine list. ◊ *177 Tremont St • Map P4 • 617 778 6841 • Closed lunch • No reservations • $$$*

8 The Oceanaire Seafood Room
This former bank retains its marble glamour in its current role as an outstanding seafood restaurant. ◊ *40 Court St • Map Q3 • 617 742 2277 • $$$$*

9 Umbria Prime
Top American beef and New England seafood are prepared with Italian panache in the glitzy Financial District. ◊ *295 Franklin St • Map R3 • 617 338 1000 • Closed Sun • $$$$$*

10 Grotto
Hearty Italian dishes, such as sweet potato ravioli with roasted chestnuts, make for luxury dining on a budget in a brick-walled underground setting.
◊ *37 Bowdoin St • Map N3 • 617 227 3434 • $$$*

> **Note:** *Unless otherwise specified, restaurants are open lunch Mon–Fri, dinner Mon–Sat*

Left **Beach Street, Chinatown** Right **Victorian townhouses, South End**

Chinatown, the Theater District, & South End

BOSTON'S COMPACT CHINATOWN *is the third most populous Chinese neighborhood in the US, concentrating a wealth of Asian experience in a small patch of real estate. Theater-goers find the proximity of Chinatown to the Theater District a boon for pre- and post-show dining. The Theater District itself is among the liveliest in the US, and its architecturally distinctive playhouses are nearly always active, often with local productions. Adjoining the Theater District to the south is South End, once an immigrant tenement area and now Boston's most diverse neighborhood by race, cultural background, and sexual orientation. The country's largest historical district of Victorian townhouses, South End has been undergoing gentrification since the 1980s and today is home to a burgeoning and energetic club, café, and restaurant scene.*

🔟 Attractions

1. Wang Theatre
2. Boston Center for the Arts
3. Tremont Street
4. Beach Street & Chinatown
5. Piano Row
6. South Station
7. Holy Cross Cathedral
8. Villa Victoria
9. Union Park Square
10. Southwest Corridor Park

Sign, Theater District

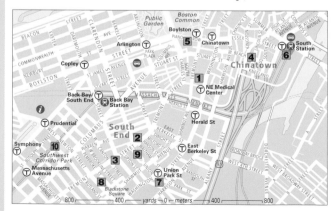

For bargain tickets and theater deals See p142

1 Wang Theatre

With a theater modeled on the Paris Opera House and a foyer inspired by the Palace of Versailles, the opulent Wang Theatre (opened 1925) is a grand venue for touring musicals, blockbuster concerts, and local productions *(see p52)*.

2 Boston Center for the Arts

The massive Cyclorama building is the centerpiece of the BCA, a performing and visual arts complex dedicated to nurturing new talent. The center provides studio space to about 40 artists, and its Mills Gallery mounts rotating visual arts exhibitions. The BCA's four theaters, home to four companies, host avant-garde productions of dance, theater, and performance art *(see p52)*.

3 Tremont Street

The section of Tremont Street between East Berkeley and Massachusetts Avenue is the social and commercial heart of the South End. Many of the handsome brick and brownstone townhouses have been restored to circa-1890 perfection, some with a boutique or café added at street level; others remain boarded up and awaiting renovation. The liveliest corner of the South End is the intersection of Tremont with Clarendon and Union Park streets, where the

Grand Lobby, Wang Theatre

Boston Center for the Arts and a plethora of restaurants and cafés create a compact entertainment and dining district. ◈ *Map N5–M6*

4 Beach Street & Chinatown

As the periphery of ethnic Chinatown becomes increasingly homogenized, Beach Street remains the purely Chinese heart of the neighborhood, home to the traditional apothecaries and other merchants who serve a primarily immigrant population. An ornate Dragon Gate at the base of Beach Street creates a ceremonial entrance to Chinatown. The wall behind the adjacent small park is painted with a dreamy mural of a Chinese sampan boat. ◈ *Map P5*

Contemporary city mural, Chinatown

 For information on culinary tours of Chinatown **See p137**

Piano Row
5 In the late 19th century, the HQs of leading piano makers Steinert, Vose, Starck, Mason and Hamlin, and Wurlitzer were located on the section of Boylston Street facing Boston Common, giving the block (now a historic district) its nickname as Piano Row. Nearly a century later, those Beaux Arts buildings still echo with music. The Colonial Theatre, its ornate interior fully restored to the sumptuous 1900 original, is an active venue for drama and musicals, while Boylston Place is a small-scale club and nightlife center. ✪ Map N4

Colonial Theatre, Piano Row

Detail, Colonial Theatre

South Station
6 A brick temple to mass transportation, the Neo-Classical Revival South Station was erected in 1898 at the height of rail travel in the US, and was once the country's busiest train station. Following extensive restoration in 1989, it now serves as an Amtrak terminal for trains from the south and west of the city, as well as a "T" stop and a social and commercial center with a lively food court and occasional lunchtime concerts. ✪ Map Q5

Holy Cross Cathedral
7 Holy Cross, the largest Roman Catholic church in Massachusetts, acts as the seat of the archbishop of Boston. The cathedral was constructed in 1875 (on the site of the municipal gallows) to serve the largely Irish-American workers who lived in the adjoining shantytown. Today the congregation is principally of Hispanic origin. Of note are the magnificent stained glass windows, which include rare colored glass imported from Munich in the 19th century, and the powerful Hook & Hastings organ, which seems to make every piece of Roxbury puddingstone in the building reverberate. ✪ 1400 Washington St • Map F6 • 617 542 5682 • open 9am–3pm daily

Villa Victoria
8 Villa Victoria is a virtually self-contained, primarily Hispanic neighborhood that grew out of a unique collaboration among Puerto Rican community activists, flexible city planners, and visionary architects. With its low-rise buildings, narrow streets, and mom-and-pop stores, Villa Victoria replicates the feel of Puerto Rican community life. At its heart, the Center for the Arts sponsors classes

South Station

Note: South End's Festival Betances (third weekend in July) is a celebration of Puerto Rican culture. Call 617 927 1707 for information

Stained glass, Center for Latino Arts, Villa Victoria

and exhibitions. In mid-July the center runs the Latino arts and cultural celebration, Festival Betances. ◈ *Area bounded by Shawmut Ave, Tremont St, W Newton St, & W Brookline St • Map F* ◈ *Center for the Arts: 85 W Newton St • 617 927 1707 • www.villavictoriaarts.org*

Union Park Square
Constructed between 1857 and 1859, this small park surrounded by English-style brick row houses was built to contrast with the French-inspired grid layout of nearby Back Bay. Graced with lovely trees and fountains and verdant with a thick mat of grass, the square was one of the first areas in the South End to be gentrified. ◈ *Map F6*

Southwest Corridor Park
The first section of the five-mile (8-km) Southwest Corridor Park divides South End and Back Bay along the "T" orange line corridor. In the residential South End portion, a path strings together numerous small parks. Between Massachusetts Avenue and West Roxbury, the park broadens to include recreational amenities. ◈ *Map E6*

Exploring Chinatown & South End

Morning

Begin on Washington Street where you can peruse the exotic produce, Chinese teas, imported Asian spices and specialty foods at **C-Mart** *(see p108)*. Continue down Essex Street, ducking into Oxford Place to see the mural, *Travelers in an Autumn Landscape*, based on the famous scroll painting by the same name at the Museum of Fine Arts. The distinctive and colorful **Dragon Gate** to Chinatown stands at the corner of Edinboro Street and Beach Street, along with pagoda-style phone booths. Walk up Beach and turn right to sample the martial arts clothing and videos at **Silky Way** *(see p108)*. Then stop for a delicious lunch at **Shabu-Zen** *(see p110)*.

Afternoon

Walk down Tremont Street to the South End, or hop on the "T" two stops to Back Bay Station. Go west on Columbus Avenue to see the elaborate bronze sculptures that tell the story of escaped slave Harriet Tubman, who led many others to freedom on the Underground Railroad, a series of hiding places in non-slave states. Back at Tremont Street, visit the **Boston Center for the Arts** *(see p105)* to get a snapshot of local contemporary art at the Mills Gallery. Then, if you have extra time, take a stroll around gracious **Union Park Square** before returning to the arts center complex for dinner and live music at **Beehive** *(see p48)*. There is a good chance that local jazz artists will be playing.

Around Town – Chinatown, the Theater District & South End

Note: *More than 200 South End artists' studios open to the public in September. Call the Boston Center for the Arts (617 426 5000)*

Left **C-Mart Supermarket** Right **Lekker Home**

TOP 10 Shops

1 Tadpole
If there was ever any doubt that young families are colonizing the South End, then Tadpole's cheery selection of clothing, toys, and accessories for children dispels it. ⊗ 58 Clarendon St • Map M6

2 Chocolee Chocolates
Self-taught chocolate and pastry guru Lee Napoli sells her wares from this ultra-tiny storefront. Her chocolate-filled beignets are perhaps the best chocolate pastry ever invented. Napoli also gives classes. ⊗ 23 Dartmouth St • Map F6 • Closed Mon–Wed

3 Lekker Home
Contemporary Italian, Scandinavian, and German home design are the highlights of this emporium, which offers the latest trends in homeware. ⊗ 1317 Washington St • Map G6 • Closed Mon

4 Las Ventas
Boston's best outlet for Spanish food and cooking utensils. It sells everything from chorizo to paella pans, and is also a good source for smoked Spanish paprika and saffron. Ask for a taste of the many cheeses. ⊗ 700 Harrison Ave • Map F6

5 Silky Way
This all-purpose martial arts store carries robes, belts, books, magazines, videos, plus a few swords and other weapons. ⊗ 33 Harrison Ave • Map P5

6 Bead & Fiber
Whether you're seeking beaded jewelry, fiber art, or just the materials to make them, this shop-gallery has everything you need, including classes. ⊗ 460 Harrison Ave • Map G6 • Closed Mon

7 Motley
A constantly changing assortment of goods reflects the tastes of the moment in this trend-setting South End store. Browse for a personal indulgence or a gift. ⊗ 623 Tremont St • Map F6

8 C-Mart Supermarket
This compact market offers vegetables, tropical fruits, and packaged foods essential for cuisines from Singapore to Seoul. ⊗ 692 Washington St • Map P5

9 okw
Fashion designer Waheeda Ali-Salaam brings 21st-century pizzazz to classic women's clothing and accessories. Look for the ever-popular "interview suits." ⊗ 234 Clarendon St, 2nd floor • Map F4 • Closed Sun

10 Syrian Grocery Importing Company
Harking back to the South End's days as a Middle Eastern immigrant neighborhood, this grocery sells southern and eastern Mediterranean essentials, from preserved lemons to rare Moroccan argan oil. ⊗ 270 Shawmut Ave • Map G5 • Closed Mon

Note: Unless otherwise specified, shops are open daily

Left **Delux Café** Center **Wally's Café** Right **Venu**

🔟 Nightclubs & Bars

1 Gypsy Bar
The colorful and sophisticated bar up front becomes a glamorous dance scene in the back. ✆ 116 Boylston St • Map N5 • 617 482 7799 • Closed Sun–Tue • Adm

2 Royale
This massive two-story dance hall occasionally morphs into a live-performance concert venue for touring acts. ✆ 279 Tremont St • Map P5 • 617 338 7699 • Closed Sun–Thu • Adm

3 Wally's Café
Exhale before you squeeze in the door at Wally's. This thin, chock-full sliver of a room is one of the best jazz bars in Boston, and has been since 1944.
✆ 427 Massachusetts Ave • Map E6

4 The Estate
Theater District alley's largest dance space throbs with the beats of house DJs and twice-weekly girl-band performances. Sunday night is a raucous gay scene. ✆ 1 Boylston Place • Map N4

5 Delux Café
Cheap drinks and an Elvis shrine lend an edge to the trendy scene here. It's good clean fun for hipster grandchildren of the beatniks (see p46). ✆ 100 Chandler St • Map M6 • Closed Sun

6 Toro
Barcelona-style tapas complement an all-Spanish wine list and a select group of creative cocktails with names like Verdad y Amor (Truth and Love). ✆ 1704 Washington St • Map F6

7 Venu
Music varies each night of the week, but it's always the same Prada-Armani-Versace-clad crowd. The Art Deco bar makes for a beautiful look. ✆ 100 Warrenton St • Map N5 • Closed Mon & Wed

8 Jacque's Cabaret
This two-level pioneer drag-queen bar features female impersonators on weekdays and edgy rock bands on weekends. ✆ 79 Broadway • Map N5 • Adm

9 28 Degrees
Small plates and big martinis fuel this stylish South End spot where the electronica never stops. ✆ 1 Appleton St • Map G5

10 The Butcher Shop
A full-service butcher shop and wine bar pairs house-made sausages, salami, and foie gras terrine with Old World wines of Italy, France, and Spain by the glass or bottle. A full menu is offered at mealtimes. ✆ 552 Tremont St • Map F6

Note: Most bars stop serving at around 1am from Sun–Thu, around 2am on weekends

Left **Restaurant sign, Chinatown** Right **Emperor's Garden**

TOP 10 Asian Restaurants

1 East Ocean City
Select your fish from the tanks near the front and ask the chef to recommend a dish.
◈ *27 Beach St • Map P5 • 617 542 2504 • No DA • $$*

2 New Shanghai
Typical southern Chinese fare is available, but best bets are lusty northern dishes like duck tea-smoked in a wok, spicy Sichuan whole fish, or Mongolian beef. ◈ *21 Hudson St • Map H5 • 617 338 0732 • $*

3 Emperor's Garden
Dim sum in this historical opera house is a theatrical experience. Note that most southern Chinese dishes are large and best shared. ◈ *690 Washington St • Map P5 • 617 482 8898 • $$*

4 Penang
Nominally "pan-Asian," Penang has a chiefly Malay menu, ranging from inexpensive noodle staples to more contemporary concoctions. ◈ *685 Washington St • Map N5 • 617 451 6372 • $$*

5 Hei La Moon
Huge, rather formal pan-Chinese restaurant on the Leather District side of Atlantic Avenue. Attracts a large crowd for weekend morning dim sum. ◈ *88 Beach St • Map Q5 • 617 338 8813 • $$*

6 Taiwan Cafe
The typically Taiwanese overbright cafeteria look should not deter aficionados of authentic, adventurous dishes like spicy pig ears and jellyfish. ◈ *34 Oxford St • Map P5 • 617 426 8181 • No credit cards • No DA • $*

7 Ginza
Fabulous maki rolls and superb sushi and sashimi make this a Japanese late-night favorite. ◈ *4 Tyler St • Map H5 • 617 338 2261 • $$*

8 Xinh Xinh
Great family-run Vietnamese pho and noodle shop, popular with both immigrants and students from the adjacent Tufts Medical Center. Take-out available. ◈ *7 Beach St • Map P5 • 617 422 0501 • $*

9 Dumpling Café
This casual spot sells several varieties of dumpling made fresh daily, alongside delicacies such as dishes using duck tongue. ◈ *695 Washington St • Map G5 • 617 338 8858 • $$*

10 Shabu-Zen
Choose your meats and vegetables and your cooking liquid, then swish away to nirvana. ◈ *16 Tyler St • Map P5 • 617 292 8828 • No DA • $*

Note: *Saturday and Sunday are the big days for dim sum in Chinatown*

Price Categories

For a three course
meal for one with half
a bottle of wine (or
equivalent meal), taxes,
and extra charges.

$	under $30
$$	$30–$45
$$$	$45–$60
$$$$	$60–$75
$$$$$	over $75

Left **Aquitaine**

🔟 Restaurants

Hamersley's Bistro
The French provincial dishes are both simple and sophisticated. ◈ 553 Tremont St • Map F5 • 617 423 2700 • Closed lunch • $$$$$

Myers + Chang
Clever reinventions of classic Chinese dishes, such as lemon shrimp dumplings; also vegetarian-friendly. Sake-based cocktails with guava and lychee are a big hit. ◈ 1145 Washington St • Map G6 • 617 542 5200 • $$

El Centro
Authentic Mexican food from a Sonoran chef emphasizes fresh flavors and serves authentic tamales and tortillas made from scratch. It is bustling on weekends. ◈ 472 Shawmut Ave • Map F6 • 617 262 5708 • $

Tremont 647
Chef Andy Husbands' New American cooking favors big portions, bold flavors, and lots of smoke with the meat. ◈ 647 Tremont St • Map F6 • 617 266 4600 • Closed lunch Mon–Sat • $$$

Les Zygomates
French bistro fare, 30 wines by the glass, and live jazz. ◈ 129 South St • Map Q5 • 617 541 5108 • Closed Sun • $$$$

Coppa
Small, Italian-inspired plates make Coppa perfect for grazing while sipping glasses of wine and basking in the romantic ambience. ◈ 252 Shawmut Ave • Map F6 • 617 391 0902 • Closed lunch Sat • $$

Sibling Rivalry
Chefs Bob and David Kinkead offer individual interpretations of a main ingredient on dueling contemporary American menus. ◈ 525 Tremont St • Map F6 • 617 338 5338 • Closed lunch • $$$$

Masa
Refined New American dishes with southwestern accents are complemented by killer margaritas, colorful decor, and good wines. ◈ 439 Tremont St • Map N6 • 617 338 8884 • Closed lunch • $$$

Market
Foodies flock to the W Hotel to sample John-Georges Vongerichten's cross-cultural, eclectic cuisine. ◈ 100 Stuart St • Map N5 • 617 310 6790 • $$$$$

Aquitaine
A Parisian-style bistro popular for its snazzy wine bar and its French market cooking. Black truffle vinaigrette makes Aquitaine's steak-frites Boston's best. ◈ 569 Tremont St • Map F5 • 617 424 8577 • Closed lunch Mon–Fri • $$$$

Note: Unless otherwise specified, all restaurants are open daily for lunch and dinner

Left **Photographic Resource Center, Boston University** Center **Heron, Back Bay Fens** Right **Jordan Hall**

Kenmore & the Fenway

ON DAYS WHEN THE RED SOX *are playing a home baseball game at Fenway Park, Kenmore Square is packed with fans. By night, Kenmore becomes the jump-off point for a night of dancing, drinking, and socializing at clubs on or near Lansdowne Street. Yet for all of Kenmore's genial rowdiness, it is also the gateway into the sedate parkland of the Back Bay Fens and the stately late 19th- and early 20th-century buildings along The Fenway. The Fenway neighborhood extends all the way southeast to Huntington Avenue, aka the "Avenue of the Arts," which links key cultural centers such as Symphony Hall, Huntington Theatre, Museum of Fine Arts, Massachusetts College of Art and Design, and the not-to-be-missed Isabella Stewart Gardner Museum along a tree-lined boulevard.*

Symphony Hall

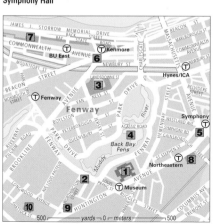

Attractions

1. Museum of Fine Arts
2. Isabella Stewart Gardner Museum
3. Fenway Park
4. Back Bay Fens
5. Symphony Hall
6. Kenmore Square
7. Boston University
8. Jordan Hall
9. Massachusetts College of Art and Design Galleries
10. Warren Anatomical Museum

Note: Take the E branch of the green line for the museums along Huntington Avenue

1 Museum of Fine Arts

One of the most comprehensive fine arts museums in the country, the MFA is especially renowned for its collections of French Impressionism and of ancient Egyptian and Nubian art and artifacts. Its

Back Bay Fens

Asian art holdings are said to be the largest in the US (see pp22–5).

2 Isabella Stewart Gardner Museum

This Fenway museum, in a faux Venetian palace, represents the exquisite personal tastes of its founder, Isabella Stewart Gardner, who was one of the country's premier art collectors at the end of the 19th century (see pp28–9).

3 Fenway Park

Built in 1912, the home field of the Boston Red Sox is the oldest surviving park in major league baseball, and aficionados insist that it's also the finest. An odd-shaped parcel of land gives the intimate park quirky features, such as the high, green-painted wall in left field, affectionately known as "the Green Monster." Although previous owners threatened to abandon Fenway, the current ones have enlarged the park to accommodate the

Fenway Park

many loyal Sox fans. Behind-the-scenes tours of the park include areas normally closed to the public, like the dugouts and private boxes. ⊗ 4 Yawkey Way • Map D5 • 617 267 1700 for tickets, 617 226 6666 for tours • Tours year-round: 9am–5pm daily (last tour 4 hours before game time) • Adm • www.redsox.mlb.com

4 Back Bay Fens

This lush ribbon of grassland, marshes, and stream banks follows Muddy River and forms one link in the Emerald Necklace of parks (see p15). The enclosed James P. Kelleher Rose Garden in the center of the Fens provides a perfect spot for quiet contemplation. A path runs from Kenmore Square to the museums and galleries on Huntington Avenue, which makes a pleasant short cut through the Fens. ⊗ Bounded by Park Dr & The Fenway • Map D5–D6

5 Symphony Hall

The restrained, elegant Italian Renaissance exterior of this 1900 concert hall barely hints at what is considered to be the acoustic perfection of the interior hall as designed by Harvard physics professor Walter Clement Sabine. Home of the Boston Symphony Orchestra, the hall's 2,361 seats are usually sold out for their classical concerts, as well as for the lighter Boston Pops (see p52).

For more on Boston's performing arts venues **See pp52–3**

Kenmore Square

6 Kenmore Square
Largely dominated by Boston University, Kenmore Square is now being transformed from a student ghetto into an extension of upmarket Back Bay, losing some of its funky character but gaining élan in the process. As the public transportation gateway to Fenway Park, the square swarms with baseball fans and sidewalk vendors, rather than students, on game days. The most prominent landmark of the square is the CITGO sign, its 5,878 glass tubes pulsing with red, white, and blue neon from dusk until midnight. *Time* magazine designated this sign an "objet d'heart" because it was so beloved by Bostonians that they prevented its dismantling in 1983. ◈ *Map D5*

7 Boston University
Founded as a Methodist Seminary in 1839, Boston University was chartered as a university in 1869. Today it enrolls approximately 28,000 students from all 50 states and some 125 countries. The scattered colleges and schools were consolidated at the Charles River Campus in 1966. Both sides of Commonwealth Avenue are lined with distinctive university buildings and sculptures. The Howard Gotlieb Archival Research Center is big on the memorabilia of show biz figures, displayed on a rotating basis. Artifacts include Gene Kelly's Oscar and a number of Bette Davis's film scripts. It also exhibits selections from its holdings of rare manuscripts and books. The Photographic Resource Center, a focus for Boston's considerable photographic community, frequently mounts challenging exhibitions of local and international photographers. ◈ *Howard Gotlieb Archival Research Center: 771 Commonwealth Ave • Map C4 • 617 353 3696 • Exhibit rooms open 9am–3:30pm Mon–Fri • Free* ◈ *Photographic Resource Center: 832 Commonwealth Ave • Map C5 • 617 975 0600 • Open Sep–Jun: 10am–5pm Tue–Fri • Call for weekend and off-season schedule • Adm*

Mugar Memorial Library, Boston University

8 Jordan Hall
The New England Conservatory of Music's 1,013-seat concert hall opened in 1903 and underwent an $8.2 million restoration in 1995. Musicians frequently praise its acoustics, heralding Jordan "the Stradivarius of concert halls." Hundreds of free classical concerts are performed at this National Historic Landmark hall every year *(see p52)*.

Paine Gallery, Massachusetts College of Art

Massachusetts College of Art and Design Galleries

The Paine and Bakalar galleries in the South Building of the Massachusetts College of Art mount some of Boston's most dynamic exhibitions of contemporary visual art. It is the only independent state-supported art college in the US and exhibitions tend to emphasize avant-garde experimentation as well as social commentary and documentary. Ⓢ 621 Huntington Ave • Map D6 • 617 879 7333 • Open noon–6pm Mon–Sat (to 8pm Wed) • Free • www.massart.edu

Warren Anatomical Museum

Established in 1847 from the private holdings of Dr. John Collins Warren, this museum contains the former anatomical teaching collections of the Harvard Medical School, including clinical examples of rare deformities and diseases. Among the displays are several delicate skeletons of stillborn conjoined twins. Ⓢ 10 Shattuck St • Map C6 • 617 432 6196 • Open 9am–5pm Mon–Fri • Free

A Day of the Arts

Afternoon

🕐 Take the green line "T" (B train) to Boston University Central and make your way to the **Howard Gotlieb Archival Research Center**, part of Boston University, for a glimpse of Fred Astaire's dancing shoes and other show business ephemera. Then head west toward **Kenmore Square** to explore the stores, including the encyclopedic Boston University Bookstore (660 Beacon St), directly under the CITGO sign. Stroll along Brookline Avenue to **Fenway Park** for a tour of the stadium (see p113) and then take Yawkey Way to the **Back Bay Fens** (see p113), where you can rest beneath the wings of the angel on the Veteran's Memorial. Continue to the **Museum of Fine Arts** (see pp22–5) to view the outstanding art collections – from ancient Egyptian artifacts to contemporary installations. Afterwards, follow The Fenway three blocks left to continue your immersion in art at the **Isabella Stewart Gardner Museum** (see pp28–9). Take a break in the "living room" of the museum's Renzo Piano-designed wing, then grab a bite to eat at classy **Café G** (see p117).

Evening

You can pack in a full evening of entertainment by taking in a recital at **Jordan Hall** (see p52). When the final applause has died down, head to **Jillian's** entertainment complex (see p116) and round off the night with billiards, bowling, and dancing into the very early hours.

Left **Cask 'n Flagon** Center **Jerry Remy's** Right **Church**

TOP 10 Nightclubs & Bars

1 Church
Live local bands Wednesday to Saturday and DJ action on Sunday make the halls of this 225-person room reverberate all through the Fenway. ❧ 69 Kilmarnock St • Map D6

2 An Tua Nua
There is a range of entertainment at this nominally Irish bar and lounge near Boston University, including country music, salsa lessons, and a weekly Goth night. ❧ 835 Beacon St • Map C5

3 Game On!
Wall-to-wall TVs are tuned to every game that's on anywhere in the country at this bar in a corner of Fenway Park. A prime spot for sports fans to eat, drink, and cheer. ❧ 82 Lansdowne St • Map D5

4 Cask 'n Flagon
At Fenway's premier sports bar, fans hoist a cold one and debate the merits of the Sox manager's latest tactics. ❧ 62 Brookline Ave • Map D5 • Closed Sun

5 Boston Beer Works
This cavernous brew pub specializes in lighter American ales and serves giant plates of ribs and chicken that can easily feed two ravenous Red Sox fans. ❧ 61 Brookline Ave • Map D5

6 Jerry Remy's Sports Bar & Grill
Red Sox broadcaster and former baseball player, Jerry Remy, set his jovial sports bar strategically between Back Bay and Fenway Park. ❧ 1265 Boylston St • Map E5

7 Audubon Circle
Close enough to Fenway Park to drop by after the game, Audubon Circle is a quiet neighborhood bar and grill with good food, beer, and a thoughtful wine list. ❧ 836 Beacon St • Map D5

8 Cornwall's Pub
Offering the very best of both worlds, Cornwall's is a British-style pub with good beer and food, but the bartenders also understand baseball. ❧ 654 Beacon St • Map D5

9 Hawthorne
Cocktails and champagnes star in this upscale lounge for Kenmore Square adults who would rather converse than yell. ❧ Hotel Commonwealth, 500 Commonwealth Ave • Map D5

10 Jillian's
Set behind Fenway Park, this entertainment complex features a choice of bars and the popular dance club, Tequila Rain. ❧ 145 Ipswich St • Map D5

Note: Unless otherwise specified, nightclubs and bars are open nightly

Price Categories

For a three course meal for one with half a bottle of wine (or equivalent meal), taxes and extra charges.

$	under $30
$$	$30–$45
$$$	$45–$60
$$$$	$60–$75
$$$$$	over $75

Left **Eastern Standard**

🔟 Restaurants

**Citizen Public House**
Craft beers, 100 whiskeys, excellent cocktails, and great pub food make Citizen a top neighborhood spot. ◈ *1310 Boylston St • Map E5 • 617 450 9000 • $$*

Elephant Walk
Chef Nadsa de Monteiro has shown just how sophisticated Cambodian food can be. Served in an airy bamboo-trimmed room. ◈ *900 Beacon St • Map C5 • 617 247 1500 • Closed lunch Sat & Sun • $$*

Symphony 8
The gastropub menu here excels in simple dishes (macaroni cheese, stout-braised short ribs). Full Irish breakfast served all day. ◈ *8 Westland Ave • Map E5 • 617 267 1200 • $*

UBurger
What a concept – fast food, but made to order! With over two dozen toppings you can truly customize your burger. ◈ *636 Beacon St • Map D5 • 617 536 0448 • $*

Trattoria Toscana
An intimate, 20 seat restaurant offering hearty Tuscan cooking. A popular place with couples. ◈ *130 Jersey St • Map D6 • 617 247 9508 • Closed lunch • $$$*

Eastern Standard
Buttoned-down versions of Continental classics have some hidden surprises on this menu, such as magnificent salt-cod fritters and Boston cream pie. ◈ *528 Commonwealth Ave • Map D5 • 617 532 9100 • $$$$*

Café G
Superb light fare, rich desserts, and fine wines complete a visit to the Isabella Stewart Gardner Museum *(see pp28–9).* ◈ *280 Fenway • Map D6 • 617 566 1088 • Closed dinner, Mon • $*

Sweet Cheeks
Chef-owner Tiffani Faison is crazy about great barbecue food. Order pork belly by the pound and drink sweet tea from Mason jars. ◈ *1301 Boylston St • Map E5 • 617 266 1300 • $*

La Verdad
This great taqueria in Jillian's complex is the real deal and aims to make the Latin American Red Sox players feel right at home. ◈ *1 Lansdowne St • Map D5 • 617 351 2580 • $$*

Petit Robert Bistro
Star chef Jackie Robert revolutionized Boston fine dining with this Parisian-style bistro, serving *cassoulet*, duck confit, *tarte tatin*, and fine wine by the glass. ◈ *468 Commonwealth Ave • Map D4 • 617 375 0699 • $$*

Left **Mural, Inman Square** Center **Musician, Harvard Square** Right **Museum of Science**

Cambridge & Somerville

HARVARD MAY HOLD CAMBRIDGE'S *undeniable claim to worldwide fame, but that is not to diminish the city's vibrant neighborhoods, superb restaurants, unique shops, and colorful bars lying just beyond the school's gates. Harvard Square, with its international newsstands, name-brand shopping, and numerous coffee houses, is a heady mix of urban bohemia and Main Street USA. And despite its 350-plus years, Cambridge is one of the most youthful cities in the country, welcoming tens of thousands of college students to Harvard, the Massachusetts Institute of Technology (MIT), and a handful of other schools every fall. To the northwest, the heavily residential city of Somerville is distinguished by its tightly knit European-style squares, where tourists seldom tread and local character abounds.*

Harvard Square

Attractions

1. Harvard University
2. Harvard Art Museums
3. Peabody & Natural History Museums
4. Charles River Banks
5. Museum of Science
6. Davis Square
7. Inman Square
8. Longfellow House
9. Cambridge Multicultural Arts Center
10. Massachusetts Institute of Technology (MIT)

Note: Cambridge and Somerville are served by the "T" red line

1 Harvard University

While its stellar reputation might suggest visions of ivory towers in the sky, Harvard is a surprisingly accessible, welcoming place. Too often, visitors limit themselves to what is visible from the Yard: Massachusetts Hall, the Widener Library, maybe University Hall. But with top-notch museums, the eclectic Harvard Square, and daring performing arts spaces such as the Loeb Drama Center and Memorial Hall's Sanders Theater *(see p52)* lying just beyond the university, Harvard provides every incentive to linger a while *(see pp16–19)*.

2 Harvard Art Museums

Harvard has some of the world's finest collegiate art collections, which are usually displayed in three separate museums. However, during extensive renovation work to the Fogg and Busch-Reisinger buildings, which will continue until fall 2014, highlights from all three museums will be on display at the Sackler Museum. Visitors will enjoy the surprising juxtapositions of Chinese bronzes, Greek vases, medieval altarpieces, and German expressionist paintings *(see pp16–19)*. ✪ Map B1 ✪ Sackler Museum, 485 Broadway • 617 495 9400 • Open 10am–5pm Tue–Sat • Adm • www.harvard.edu/museums

Memorial Hall, Harvard University

3 Peabody & Natural History Museums

Its ongoing commitment to research aside, the Peabody excels at illustrating how interactions between distinct cultures have in turn affected peoples' lives and livelihoods. Its North American Indian exhibit displays artifacts that reflect the aftermath of encounters between white Europeans and Native Americans. The Natural History museum delves even deeper in time, exhibiting eons-old natural wonders *(see pp16–19)*. ✪ Peabody Museum: 11 Divinity Ave • Map B1 • 617 496 1027 • Open 9am–5pm daily • Adm ✪ Natural History Museum: 26 Oxford St • Map B1 • 617 495 3045 • Open 9am–5pm daily • Adm • www.harvard.edu/museums

4 Charles River Banks

Whether you're cheering the rowers of the Head of the Charles Regatta *(see p55)* or watching the "T" cross Longfellow Bridge through a barrage of snowflakes, the banks of the Charles River offer a fantastic vantage point for taking in Boston's celebrated scenes. On summer Sundays, the adjacent Memorial Drive becomes a sea of strollers, joggers, and rollerbladers *(see p123)*. ✪ Map B2–F3

Charles River Banks

Note: Free tours of Harvard Yard depart from Holyoke Center (1350 Massachusetts Ave, 617 495 1573)

Local Stages
The performing arts form an integral part of the character of Cambridge and Somerville. The ornate Somerville Theater *(see p53)* draws nationally recognized musical acts, while the Loeb Drama Center *(see p53)* stages The American Repertory Theatre's daring, top-notch productions. And Harvard student-produced pieces grace the Hasty Pudding Theatre's stage (12 Holyoke St, Cambridge, 617 495 5205).

Museum of Science
Exploring the cosmos in the Hayden Planetarium, hitting the high notes on a musical staircase, experiencing larger-than-life IMAX films in the Mugar Omni Theater – the Museum of Science knows how to make learning enjoyable. In addition to these attractions, the museum hosts blockbuster shows like *Harry Potter: The Exhibit*. Live presentations take place throughout the day.
⊗ Science Park • Map N1 • 617 723 2500 • Open 9am–5pm Mon–Thu, Sat & Sun (to 7pm Jul–Sep), 9am–9pm Fri • Adm • www.mos.org

Davis Square
With its cooler-than-thou coffee shops, lively bar scene, affordable restaurants, and the renowned Somerville Theater *(see p53)*, Davis Square, Somerville stands as the metro area's most desirable neighborhood for many young Bostonians. And with prestigious Tufts University just a 10-minute walk away, the square's youthful spirit is in a constant state of replenishment.

Inman Square
Oft-overlooked Inman Square is possibly Cambridge's best-kept secret. Boasting such renowned restaurants and cafés as the East Coast Grill and 1369, ace jazz club Ryles *(see p49)*, plus Christina's delectable ice creams *(see p45)*, Inman handsomely rewards those willing to go out of their way to experience a real-deal Cambridge neighborhood. ⊗ Map D1

Longfellow House
Poet Henry Wadsworth Longfellow can be credited with helping to shape Boston's – and America's – collective identity. His poetic documentation of Paul Revere's midnight ride *(see p38)* immortalized both him and his subject. In 1837, Longfellow took up residence in this house, a few blocks from Harvard Yard. He was not the house's first illustrious resident. General George Washington headquartered and planned the 1776 siege of Boston in these rooms. The building is preserved with furnishings of Longfellow's and Washington's heydays, and houses the poet's archives. ⊗ 105 Brattle St • Map A1 • 617 876 4491 • Open Jun–Oct: tours 10:30am–4pm Wed–Sun • www.nps.gov/long

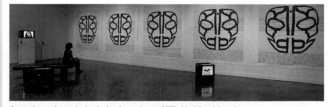

Amorales vs Amorales by Carlos Amorales, at MIT's List Visual Arts Center

Museum of Science

9 Cambridge Multicultural Arts Center

Housed in a beautiful 19th-century courthouse, the CMAC presents performance and visual art exhibitions which promote cross-cultural exchange. A unique feature is the encouragement of dialogue between audience and artist after performances and openings. ◈ *41 2nd St • Map F2 • 617 577 1400 • Open 10:30am–6pm Mon–Fri • Free*

10 Massachusetts Institute of Technology (MIT)

Not to be outdone by its irrepressible Ivy League neighbor, MIT has been the country's leading technical university since its founding in 1861. This school of improbable theorems and calculator-toting world shapers offers many places of interest. Its List Visual Arts Center exhibits work that comments on technology or employs it in fresh, surprising ways. Also of note is the MIT Museum, with its interactive exhibits on artificial intelligence, holography, and the world's first computers. ◈ *77 Massachusetts Ave • Map D3 • 617 253 4795* ◈ *List Visual Arts Center: 20 Ames St, Cambridge • 617 253 4680 • Open noon–6pm Tue–Sun (to 8pm Thu) • Free* ◈ *MIT Museum: 265 Massachusetts Ave • 617 253 5927 • Open 10am–5pm daily • Adm • www.mit.edu*

The Cambridge Curriculum

Morning

Call the Museum of Science early to learn what features are playing at the Omni Theater and book tickets over the phone for an afternoon show. Then begin your morning with a stack of pancakes at Davis Square's legendary **Rosebud Diner**. Next, ride the "T" inbound to Harvard and head straight to **Out of Town News** (0 Harvard Sq) to peruse their mind-boggling selection of international magazines and newspapers. Take time in Harvard Yard *(see p16)* to stop at the **John Harvard Statue** *(see p16)*, in front of Charles Bulfinch's University Hall, to scrutinize its "three lies." Then return to Massachusetts Avenue and walk east to Quincy Street for a sampling of highlights from the University art collections at the **Sackler Museum** *(see p17)*.

Afternoon

Head back on Massachusetts Avenue toward the square to **Bartley's Burger Cottage** (1246 Massachusetts Ave) for a lunch of freshly prepared specialty burgers and irresistible sweet potato fries. You can fully digest on the 20 minute "T" ride to Science Park. Head to the **Museum of Science's** Omni Theater and claim your tickets. After an exhilarating, in-your-face feature, retrace your steps toward Cambridge on the "T" as far as Central Square where you can sit back and enjoy a refreshing glass of Guinness in the convivial atmosphere at **The Field** (20 Prospect St).

Note: MIT is a scenic 20-minute walk from Downtown Boston across Longfellow Bridge

121

Left **Games People Play** Right **Retro goods at Abodeon**

TOP 10 Offbeat Shops

1 Black Ink
From aluminum ring binders to spring-clip photo frames, MUT features quirky items you didn't know you couldn't live without.
◎ 5 Brattle St, Cambridge • Map B1

2 Revolution Books
Che Guevara and Mao Tse Tung are alive and well here. You can read up on Communism and purchase left-leaning T-shirts, posters, buttons, and stickers.
◎ 1158 Massachusetts Ave, Cambridge • Map B2 • Closed Sun & Mon

3 Abodeon
Abodeon stocks home furnishings of the decidedly retro variety. Items include 1940s rolling chaise longes, vintage cocktail services, and even the occasional Wurlitzer jukebox.
◎ 1731 Massachusetts Ave, Cambridge

4 Magpie
Packed with handmade crafts, art by local artists, and goods from indie designers, this hipster Davis Square boutique playfully advertises "shiny things for your nest." ◎ 416 Highland Ave, Somerville

5 Hubba Hubba
If only Cambridge's Puritanical founders could have seen it: fetishist accessories, spiked belts, sexy leather corsets, and not-so-innocent toys line the shelves of this risqué Central Square boutique. ◎ 534 Massachusetts Ave, Cambridge • Map C3–D3 • Closed Sun

6 Million Year Picnic
New England's oldest comic bookstore keeps its faithful customers happy with an extensive back-issue selection, rare imports, and all the latest indie comics. ◎ 99 Mt Auburn St, Cambridge • Map B2

7 Poor Little Rich Girl
Mix and match vintage and modern at this second-hand store run by a fashion-design graduate. Some brand-new items are also for sale. ◎ 121 Hampshire St, Cambridge • Map D2 • Closed Wed

8 Games People Play
Board games, card games, role-playing games, word games, action games, puzzles... if someone plays it, Games People Play either sells it or can get it for you in a couple of days.
◎ 1100 Massachusetts Ave, Cambridge • Map B1

9 Colonial Drug
This old-fashioned pharmacy-cum-*parfumerie* features more than 1,000 hard-to-find scents that range from Aprège to Zibeline. ◎ 49 Brattle St, Cambridge • Map B1

10 Porter Exchange Mall
Take a trip to Tokyotown in this renovated 1928 Deco building, boasting a Japanese-style noodle hall and gift shops with all forms of Far Eastern ephemera. ◎ 1815 Massachusetts Ave, Cambridge

Note: Shops are open daily unless otherwise specified

Left **1369 Coffee House** Right **The Pit**

🔟 Places to Mix with the Locals

Memorial Drive
Memorial Drive is a magnet for joggers and rollerbladers. On summer Sundays, the road closes to vehicular traffic and becomes the city's best people-watching spot. ⊗ *Map B4–F3*

The Pit
On and around this sunken brick platform, street musicians, protesters, punk rockers, and uncategorizables create a scene worthy of a *Life* magazine spread. ⊗ *Bounded by JFK St & Massachusetts Ave, Cambridge • Map B1*

The Neighborhood
Sunday brunch at the Neighborhood brings throngs intent on securing seating beneath the outdoor grape arbors. Equally coveted are the house's Portuguese breakfast bread platters. ⊗ *25 Bow St, Somerville • Map D1 • 617 623 9710 • $*

1369 Coffee House
Set in the somewhat detached Inman Square, this branch of 1369 has poetry readings, mellow music, and courteous staff, which give it a neighborly atmosphere. ⊗ *1369 Cambridge St, Cambridge • Map D1 • 617 576 1369 • $*

Brattle Theater
A Harvard Square institution, the Brattle screens cinema greats daily. Rainy afternoon? Take in a 2-for-1 Fellini double feature for under $15. ⊗ *40 Brattle St, Cambridge • 617 876 6837 • Map B1*

Au Bon Pain
Every kind of Cambridge character can be found sipping coffee and munching croissants on the plaza at Holyoke Center. Top amusement? Challenging the chess masters to a speed game. ⊗ *1360 Massachusetts Ave, Cambridge • Map B1 • 617 497 9797 • $*

Improv Boston
The improvisational comedy troupe here will often explore the offbeat side of Boston life and welcomes audience participation. ⊗ *40 Prospect St, Cambridge • Map C2 • 617 576 1253*

Club Passim
The subterranean epicenter of New England's thriving folk music scene regularly welcomes nationally renowned artists. It boasts an inventive vegetarian kitchen, Veggie Planet ⊗ *47 Palmer St, Cambridge • Map B1 • 617 492 7679*

Richard Trum Playground
Summer in Somerville is epitomized by one thing: baseball at the playground. On most weeknights, you can watch energetic youngsters take their swings. ⊗ *Broadway, Somerville*

Dado Tea
This Harvard Square hangout, owned by locals, is a serene, tranquil place to settle in with an exotic cup of tea and healthy pastries, sandwiches, wraps, and salads. ⊗ *50 Church St, Cambridge • Map B1 • 617 547 0950*

Note: *All cafés are open daily*

Left **Regattabar** Right **Lizard Lounge**

🔟 Nightclubs & Bars

1 The Middle East
A live music club to rival any in New York or Los Angeles, the Middle East rocks its patrons from three stages and nourishes them with delicious kebabs and curries. ⊗ *472–480 Massachusetts Ave, Cambridge • Map D3 • 617 864 3278 • Adm*

2 Western Front
Live soul, R&B, hip-hop, Latin, and especially reggae make Western Front the alternative club for Bostonians and Cantabrigians of color. Local jazz on Wednesdays. ⊗ *343 Western Ave, Cambridge • Map B3–C3*

3 Regattabar
Befitting its location in the sleek Charles Hotel, Regattabar offers a refined yet casual setting for watching jazz giants. Shows sell out quickly. ⊗ *1 Bennett St, Cambridge • Map B2 • Closed Sun & Mon*

4 Johnny D's
Dance to live zydeco, East Coast swing, and salsa all in one night. Davis Square's – and arguably all of Boston's – home for eclectic live music. Dinner served Tuesday to Saturday. ⊗ *17 Holland St, Somerville • 617 776 2004 • Adm*

5 Trina's Starlite Lounge
A relaxed vibe, cheap beer, and diner-style food like chicken, waffles, and Sloppy Joes makes Trina's the preferred hangout for a generation of Somerville-Cambridge hipsters. ⊗ *3 Beacon St, Somerville • Map C1–D1*

6 Hong Kong
Chinese food at ground level gives way to a bustling lounge on the second floor and a raucous comedy nightclub on the third. Tuesday night features a comic magic show. ⊗ *1238 Massachusetts Ave, Cambridge • Map B2 • Comedy club closed Sun*

7 Lord Hobo
Forty draft beers, homey bistro food, and an ambitious and inventive cocktail program attract an eclectic crowd, from hipsters to software geeks. ⊗ *92 Hampshire St, Cambridge • Map D2*

8 Lizard Lounge
Just outside Harvard Square, the Lizard Lounge attracts a young, alternative rock- and folk-loving crowd with the promise of good live music and a small cover charge. ⊗ *1667 Massachusetts Ave, Cambridge • Map B1*

9 T. T. the Bear's Place
T. T.'s is a rock club in the tradition of New York's C.B.G.B.: small, dingy, and incredibly loud. Expect to sweat, expect to leave with ringing ears, and, above all, expect to rock out. ⊗ *10 Brookline St, Cambridge • Map C3*

10 River Gods
Eccentric decor, video game nights, and a hip crowd make this one of Boston's more interesting nightspots. Nightly entertainment switches between DJs and live acts. ⊗ *125 River St, Cambridge • Map C3*

 See also Beehive and Ryles **See pp48 & 49**

Price Categories

For a three course	**$** under $30
meal for one with half	**$$** $30–$45
a bottle of wine (or	**$$$** $45–$60
equivalent meal), taxes,	**$$$$** $60–$75
and extra charges.	**$$$$$** over $75

Left **Area 4**

🔟 Restaurants

1 Oleana
Chef Ana Sortun's mastery of exotic spices is clearly evident in Oleana's sumptuous Middle Eastern cuisine, served in a casually elegant dining room. ◈ *134 Hampshire St, Cambridge • Map D2 • 617 661 0505 • Closed lunch daily • $$$$*

2 Redbones
Redbones' kitchen slings some of the best barbecue north of the Carolinas, and the atmosphere could not be more emphatically Southern if it tried. ◈ *55 Chester St, Somerville • 617 628 2200 • $*

3 Rendezvous
Chef and owner Steve Johnson is a passionate champion of local produce, which he uses superbly in his creative western Mediterranean dishes at this friendly spot. Vegetarian options are always available. ◈ *501 Massachusetts Ave, Cambridge • Map C3 • 617 576 1900 • $$$$*

4 Posto
Handmade pastas, Naples-certified pizza, and wood-grilled meats and fish make Posto one of the most popular restaurants in Davis Square. ◈ *187 Elm St, Somerville • Map B2 • 617 625 0600 • Closed lunch Mon–Sat • $$*

5 Atasca
The bold flavors of Portugal are yours for the tasting at the warmly appointed, cozy Atasca. Flavorful sautées and rustic grilled dishes are just some of its many charms. ◈ *50 Hampshire St, Cambridge • Map D2 • 617 621 6991 • $$$*

6 Chez Henri
Cuba might seem an unlikely place for a French restaurant to draw inspiration, but therein lies Chez Henri's irresistible appeal. ◈ *1 Shepard St, Cambridge • Map B1 • No reservations • Closed lunch • $$$*

7 Area 4
Food is served as early as 7am at this bakery-café, and continues into the night with New American comfort food and pizzas. ◈ *500 Technology Sq, Cambridge • Map D2 • 617 758 4444 • $*

8 East by Northeast
New England produce meets modern Chinese technique in the hands of chef Phillip Tang. Bargain prices include an eight-course tasting menu for $35. ◈ *1128 Cambridge St, Cambridge • Map D2 • 617 876 0286 • Closed lunch & Mon • $$*

9 Restaurant Dante
Creative interpretations of contemporary Italian cuisine are the highlights of this refined dining room at the Royal Sonesta *(see p147)*. ◈ *40 Edwin H. Land Blvd, Cambridge • Map F3 • 617 497 4200 • $$$$*

10 Craigie On Main
Delicious meat and fish dishes are offered at this cozy venue where the menu changes daily. ◈ *853 Main St, Cambridge • Map D3 • 617 497 5511 • $$$$$*

> **Note:** Unless otherwise specified, reservations are recommended for all the above restaurants. See also Salts p40

Left **Gorilla at Franklin Park Zoo** Right **Franklin Park**

Boston South

SOUTH OF FORT POINT CHANNEL, Boston's neighborhoods of Jamaica Plain, Roxbury, Dorchester, and South Boston are a mixture of densely residential streets and leafy parklands that form part of Frederick Law Olmsted's Emerald Necklace (see p15). The lively street scenes of Boston's African-American, Latin-American, and Irish-American communities make the city's southerly neighborhoods a dynamic ethnic contrast to the more homogenized city core. Virtually ignored by tourists, Boston South is full of quirky shops, local bars, hot nightclubs, and great off-beat places to enjoy ethnic food. This area is a little harder to reach but it is worth the effort to experience a more edgy, diverse Boston that many call home.

Jamaica Pond

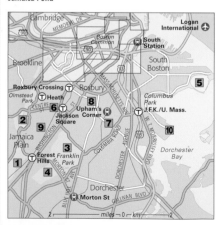

🔟 Attractions

1. Arnold Arboretum
2. Jamaica Pond
3. Franklin Park
4. Forest Hills Cemetery
5. Pleasure Bay
6. Centre Street
7. Upham's Corner
8. Dudley Square
9. Samuel Adams Brewery
10. John F. Kennedy Library & Museum

Note: For the parks and cemetery take the "T" down to Green Street or Forest Hills (orange line) **See back flap**

Arnold Arboretum

One of the US's foremost collections of temperate-zone trees and shrubs covers the peaceful 265-acre (107-ha) arboretum. Grouped in scientific fashion, they are a favorite subject for landscape painters, and a popular resource for botanists and gardeners. The world's most extensive lilac collection blooms from early May through late June, and thousands of Bostonians turn out for Lilac Sunday, in mid-May, to picnic and enjoy the peak of the *Syringa* blooms. The main flowering period of mountain laurel, azaleas, and other rhododendrons begins around Memorial Day (end of May). ⚲ *125 Arborway, Jamaica Plain • 617 524 1718*

Jamaica Pond

This 70-acre (28-ha) pond and its surrounding leafy park was landscaped by Frederick Law Olmsted to accentuate its natural glacial features and it offers an enchanting piece of countryside within the city. Locals take avidly to the 1.5-mile (2.4-km) bankside path or fish in the 90-ft- (28-m-) deep glacial kettle pond (fishing is permitted with a Massachusetts license, call 617 626 1590). The

Forest Hills Cemetery

Arnold Arboretum

boathouse rents small sail boats, kayaks, and rowboats during the summer. ⚲ *Jamaica Pond Boathouse, Jamaica Way • 617 522 5061 • open 10am–6pm daily • www.cityofboston.gov/parks*

Franklin Park

Frederick Law Olmsted considered Franklin Park the masterpiece of his Emerald Necklace *(see p15)*, but his vision of urban wilds has since been modified to more modern uses. The park boasts the second oldest municipal golf course in the US and the child-friendly Franklin Park Zoo *(see p61)*, which contrasts contemporary ecological exhibits with charming zoo architecture, such as a 1912 Oriental bird house. ⚲ *Franklin Park Rd, Dorchester • 617 265 4084*

Forest Hills Cemetery

More than 100,000 graves dot the rolling landscape in this Victorian-era "garden cemetery", one of the first of its kind. Maps available at the entrance identify graves of notable figures, including poet e e cummings and playwright Eugene O'Neill. Striking memorials include the bas-relief *Death Stays the Hand of the Artist* by Daniel Chester French, near the main entrance. ⚲ *95 Forest Hills Ave, Jamaica Plain • 617 524 0128*

Pleasure Bay

Pleasure Bay

South Boston's Pleasure Bay park encloses a pond-like cove of Boston harbor with a causeway boardwalk, where locals turn out for their daily constitutionals. Castle Island, now attached to the mainland, has guarded the mouth of Boston harbor since the first fortress, Fort Independence, was erected in 1779. A grisly murder here in 1817 inspired Edgar Allen Poe to write his short story *The Cask of Amontillado*. Anglers gather on the adjacent Steel Pier and drop bait into the midst of striped bass and bluefish runs.

Centre Street

Jamaica Plain is home to many artists, musicians, and writers as well as a substantial contingent of Boston's gay and lesbian community. Centre Street is the area's main artery and hub. There is a distinctly Latin-American flavor at the Jackson Square end, where Caribbean music shops and Cuban, Dominican, and Mexican eateries abound. At the 600 block, Centre Street morphs into an urban counter-cultural village, with design boutiques, funky second-hand stores, and small cafés and restaurants.

Upham's Corner

The area known as Upham's Corner in Dorchester was founded in 1630, and its venerable Old Dorchester Burial Ground contains ethereal carved stones from this Puritan era. Today, Upham's Corner is decidedly more Caribbean than Puritan, with small shops specializing in food, clothing, and music of the islands. The Strand Theatre, a 1918 luxury movie palace and vaudeville hall, functions as an arts center and venue for live concerts and religious revival meetings.
※ *Strand Theatre, 543 Columbia Rd, Dorchester • 617 635 1403*

Dudley Square

Roxbury's Dudley Square is the heart of African-American Boston as well as the busiest hub in Boston's public transport network. The Beaux Arts station is modeled on the great train stations of Europe. Among the square's many shops and galleries is the Hamill Gallery of Tribal Art, as much a small museum as a gallery. A few blocks from the square, the modest Georgian-style Dillaway-Thomas House

John F. Kennedy Library & Museum

Note: Take the "T" to Dudley Square for Roxbury (silver line), or to Jackson Square for Jamaica Plain (orange line) **See back flap**

reveals Roxbury's early history, including the period when it served as HQ for the Continental Army's General John Thomas during the Siege of Boston.
◈ *Hamill Gallery of Tribal Art, 2164 Washington St, Roxbury • 617 442 8204 • Open noon–6pm Thu–Sat* ◈ *Dillaway-Thomas House, 183 Roxbury St, Roxbury • 617 445 3399 • Call in advance for tour hours • Free*

Barrels, Samuel Adams Brewery

Samuel Adams Brewery

With its supply of good local water and knowledgeable German immigrants, Jamaica Plain has long been Boston's brewing center. The Boston Beer Company, creator of Samuel Adams lagers, maintains this small brewery and beer museum.
◈ *30 Germania St, Jamaica Plain • 617 368 5080 • Tours 10am–3pm Mon–Thu, 10am–5:30pm Fri, 10am–3pm Sat • Donation • www.samueladams.com*

John F. Kennedy Library & Museum

This nine-story white pyramidal building designed by I. M. Pei in 1977 stands like a billowing sail on Columbia Point. Inside, exhibits recreate the 1,000 days of the Kennedy presidency, including the Oval Office. Kennedy was the first president to grasp the power of broadcast, and video exhibits include campaign debates and coverage of Kennedy's assassination and funeral.
◈ *Columbia Point, Dorchester • 617 514 1600 • Open 9am–5pm daily • Adm • www.jfklibrary.org*

Street Heat & Pond Cool in Jamaica Plain

Afternoon

The orange line "T" will deliver you to the Latin end of Jamaica Plain's **Centre Street** at Jackson Square, where life is more Santo Domingo than downtown Boston. Head west from the station and get in the rhythm by perusing more than 10,000 titles of Caribbean and Latin music at **Franklin CD** (314 Centre St). Dominican-born owner Franklin Cabral, himself a musician, is pictured on the walls with many of Boston's Latin American Red Sox players. A promenade along Centre Street is a lesson in Latin fashion and food. Pass **El Miami** *(see p131)* and other Cubano sandwich joints, before the street doglegs left. At **J. P. Licks** (659 Centre St) order a cone of super-premium ice cream, and window-shop along Centre Street to check out the hipster thrift store **Boomerangs** (716 Centre St) for vintage clothing and home decor. Stroll up Burroughs Street and cross Jamaicaway to **Jamaica Pond** *(see p127)*, where you can walk the path around the pond, rest in the shade of a big maple tree, or rent a rowboat.

Evening

Once you have worked up a healthy appetite, return to Centre Street for a dinner of enchiladas in spicy molé sauce at **Tacos el Charro** *(see p131)*. Afterwards, walk over to the Brewery Complex on Amory to the **Milky Way Lounge** *(see p130)* and join the cool cats for a bottle of chilled beer, live music, and dancing.

Note: *For the John F. Kennedy Library and the east of the area catch the "T" to JFK/U Mass (red line)* **See back flap**

129

Left **Doyle's Café** Right **Amrhein's**

Bars & Clubs

1 Doyle's Café
The apex of Irish-American political culture, Doyle's has been serving beer since 1882, and corned beef and cabbage on Thursdays for as long as anyone can remember. Busy nightly.
◈ *3484 Washington St, Jamaica Plain*

2 Milky Way Lounge
Situated in JP's legendary Brewery Complex, Latinos and Jamaica Plain hipsters rub shoulders at the Milky Way. They come for the dancing, the latest local live bands, and the cosmopolitans.
◈ *280 Amory St, Jamaica Plain*

3 Playwright Bar
A spiffy Dublin-style pub with good food, excellent pints, and large windows that let in the sunlight and the breeze.
◈ *658 East Broadway, South Boston*

4 Dbar
The eclectic dinner menu disappears around 10pm, when Dbar morphs into a hopping, diverse nightclub where brightly colored cocktails are a specialty. Show tunes on Tuesdays, rock videos on Fridays. ◈ *1236 Dorchester Ave, Dorchester*

5 Boston Beer Garden
On weekends this watering hole is packed both inside and outside in the garden – it's a typical beer-drinking, South Boston singles scene. Modern pub food hits a fairly high mark.
◈ *734 East Broadway, South Boston*

6 Amrhein's
The vintage bar at Amrhein's – a South Boston fixture since 1890 – is reason enough to visit the 'hood. Locals debate the issue of the day over a drink or two.
◈ *80 West Broadway, South Boston*

7 Lucky's Lounge
A Fort Point Channel underground bar that swaggers with rat pack retro ambience, right down to the lounge acts and the Frank Sinatra tribute nights.
◈ *355 Congress St, South Boston*

8 Brendan Behan Pub
This classic "new" Irish pub, frequented by cheerful neighborhood types with vaguely poetic pretensions, is properly outfitted with Guinness and Murphy's on tap and live music most nights.
◈ *378 Centre St, Jamaica Plain*

9 Local 149
This South Boston neighborhood joint features 22 beers on tap, plus innumerable cans and bottles, and some of the best New American food outside of a fancy restaurant. ◈ *149 P St, South Boston*

10 Jeannie Johnston
This entertainment venue has plenty to offer, with an open mike on Thursdays, live local bands on Fridays, and karaoke on Saturdays, as well as a snug spot to sit with one of its 27 draught or bottled beers. ◈ *144 South St, Jamaica Plain*

  Note: On Sunday evenings in June, free outdoor concerts take place at Pinebank, overlooking Jamaica Pond (Jamaica Plain)

Price Categories

For a three course		
meal for one with half	**$**	under $30
a bottle of wine (or	**$$**	$30–$45
equivalent meal), taxes,	**$$$**	$45–$60
and extra charges.	**$$$$**	$60–$75
	$$$$$	over $75

Left **Tavolo**

🔟 Restaurants & Eateries

Franklin Southie
French bistro fare, like steak-frites and cassoulet, keep the tables busy at this eatery where meals are served until midnight. ◈ 152 Dorchester Ave, South Boston • 617 269 1003 • Closed lunch Mon–Sat • $

Bella Luna
The dining room adjacent to the Milky Way Lounge (see p130), Bella Luna shoots the moon with bright salads, rib-sticking Italian fare such as chicken marsala, and their signature gourmet pizzas. ◈ 280 Armory St, Jamaica Plain • 617 524 6060 • $$$

224 Boston Street
This chef-driven northern Italian trattoria is the longest lasting and most successful restaurant in the 'hood. Feast on grilled Tuscan meats and pasta dishes at half the price of North End's restaurants. ◈ 224 Boston St, Dorchester • 617 265 1217 • Closed lunch • $$

Ashmont Grill
Superchef Chris Douglass uses local produce to conjure up contemporary bistro delights. ◈ 555 Talbot Ave, Dorchester • Map D4 • 617 825 4300 • Open daily for dinner and lunch Mon–Fri, brunch Sat & Sun • $$

El Miami Restaurant
The self-proclaimed "King of the Cuban sandwiches." Check out the photos of the Latino pro baseball players who often eat here when in town. ◈ 381 Centre St, Jamaica Plain • 617 522 4644 • $

Tavolo
Superb rustic Italian cuisine emphasizes fresh market dining in this Ashmont neighborhood. ◈ 1918 Dorchester Ave, Dorchester • 617 822 1918 • Closed lunch • $

Ten Tables
This small venue really has just ten tables with an equally compact but rewarding menu, such as scallops on minted pea tendrils. ◈ 597 Centre St, Jamaica Plain • 617 524 8810 • Closed lunch • $$

Tacos el Charro
This is the best place in town for real northern Mexican food, plus it has the most complete line of Mexican beers in town. The owner plays in a mariachi band at weekends. ◈ 349 Centre St, Jamaica Plain • 617 983 9275 • Closed lunch Mon–Thu • $

Tres Gatos
This combination tapas bar and book/music store features authentic Spanish bar dishes, including imported charcuterie, along with inventive variants like roast pork belly with turnip or lamb's tongue and grits. ◈ 470 Centre St, Jamaica Plain • 617 477 4851 • $$

Blue Nile
Ethiopian home-style food celebrates fresh veggies as well as meats and fish. Teff injera, the sourdough pancakes that double as utensils, are made on the premises. ◈ 389 Centre St, Jamaica Plain • 617 522 6453 • Closed Mon • $

 Note: The seafood restaurant No Name on Fish Pier is also in this area See p42

STREETSMART

BOSTON'S TOP 10

Left **New England fall foliage** Center **US money** Right **Student card**

Planning Your Trip

1 When to Go
Boston's main tourist season is from May to October. The largest number of visitors come during the summer vacation, and in late September and early October when people flock to see the famous New England fall foliage. Hotel rooms are scarce during these periods. The second half of October offers a combination of good weather with lower accommodation rates.

2 Weather
From December to February daytime temperatures generally remain just above freezing and snow is possible. March to May is characterized by warm, sunny days alternating with showery ones. June to August is warm to hot with high humidity. September and October are mostly dry with crisp nights. November is cool and damp, with sporadic cold but sunny days. For detailed forecasts log on to www.theboston channel.com/weather.

3 Passports & Visas
All citizens of the US must show passports. Citizens of Canada, the European Union (including the UK), Australia, New Zealand, and Japan need a valid machine-readable passport and should complete the ESTA form available on-line at https://esta.cbp.dhs.gov.

A small fee is charged. Citizens of other countries must have a passport and visa, which can be obtained from a US consulate or embassy. For the latest information check on-line: www.state.gov.

4 Money
MasterCard, Visa, and American Express are accepted almost universally, and ATMs (cash machines) are located throughout the city and at Logan airport (on the departures level). It's always best to have a few dollars on arrival to pay for transportation into the city.

5 Insurance
Insurance for medical and dental care is strongly recommended, as US medical fees are costly. It is also invaluable in case of an emergency. You may have to pay for services and be reimbursed later. It's advisable to take out comprehensive insurance, which covers lost baggage, trip cancellation fees, etc.

6 Drivers License
A driver's license valid in your home country is also valid for driving in Boston and the surrounding states. Additional photo ID may be necessary to rent a vehicle.

7 What to Pack
The weather is unpredictable and can change quickly so dress in layers with a sweater or light jacket for cool summer evenings. Be sure to bring a folding umbrella, sunglasses, and comfortable walking shoes. Pack smart-casual outfits for restaurants and evening entertainment.

8 Current Adapters
US electricity is 110–120 volts, 60 cycles, and uses a polarized two-prong plug. Non-US appliances will need an adapter and a voltage converter available at airport shops and some department and electrical stores. Most laptops and travel appliances are dual voltage and many hotels have dedicated dual-voltage sockets for electric shavers.

9 Student & Senior ID
Public transit, movie theaters, most major attractions, and some hotels offer discounted rates for people 65 and older. Most museums and attractions also offer discounted admission charges for students with relevant photo ID.

10 Time Zone
Like the rest of the US east coast, Boston is in the Eastern time zone, which is GMT minus five hours. Daylight saving time begins at 2am on the second Sunday in March, and reverts to standard time at 2am on the first Sunday in November.

Left **Amtrak train** Right **Trolleys, Logan International Airport**

🔟 Arriving in Boston

1 Logan International Airport

Logan International Airport lies on an island across the inner harbor 2 miles (3.2 km) northeast of downtown. It's served by almost all major North American airlines and by most international airlines ◈ *Information: 617 561 1800 or 1-800-23-LOGAN • www.massport.com/LOGAN*

2 Connections from Logan Airport

Taxis wait at all terminals but airport fees can make a downtown trip expensive ($20–$30). The cheapest way ($2) into town is on the MBTA subway (approx. 15 minutes). Free buses connect terminals to the subway. The most scenic approach is the City Water Taxi ($10), which crosses the harbor between Logan and Atlantic Avenue ◈ *City Water Taxi: 617 422 0392 • www.citywatertaxi.com*

3 Alternate Airports

Some international charter flights and several domestic carriers use the less crowded Manchester, New Hampshire Airport, 50 miles (79 km) from Boston, and TF Green Airport, near Providence, Rhode Island, 59 miles (94.5 km) from Boston. A bus service is available in both cities. ◈ *Manchester: 603 624 6556 • www.flymanchester.com ◈ TF Green Airport: 401 737 8222 • www.pvdairport.com*

4 Customs Allowances

$100 worth of gifts, 200 cigarettes or 50 (non-Cuban) cigars, and one liter of liquor may be brought into the US without paying duty. Meat, seeds, growing plants, and fresh fruit are not allowed.

5 Immigration

Landing cards and customs declaration forms are usually distributed on the plane.

6 By Train

Amtrak trains arrive at South Station (Atlantic and Summer sts) via Back Bay station (145 Dartmouth St). There are frequent trains to New York via coastal Connecticut and Rhode Island. Services take 4–5 hours and there's also a 3-hour high-speed service. A "Downeaster" service runs to Portland, Maine. ◈ *Amtrak: 1 800 872 7245 • www.amtrak.com*

7 By Bus

Buses are the least expensive way to travel in the US. Greyhound and Peter Pan Bus Lines provide nationwide and regional New England services. All the different carriers share the South Station Bus Terminal (700 Atlantic Av). ◈ *Greyhound Bus Lines: 617 526 1800 or 1 800 231 2222 ◈ Peter Pan Bus Lines: 1 800 343 9999 or 1 888 751 8800*

8 By Ship

Cruise ships dock at Black Falcon Terminal, South Boston, which is a $10 taxi ride to Downtown. The bus service is infrequent (No. 6 from Marine Industrial Park).

9 By Car

Most major northeast highways converge on Boston, with I-95 (also known as Route 128) circumventing the city center. I-90, the Massachusetts Turnpike, comes in from the west. I-93 cuts through the city north to south as an underground expressway completed in 2004 – the commonly called "Big Dig." Watch signs carefully for exits. The purple-lit Zakim suspension bridge, connecting underground and surface highways, provides a dramatic northern gateway to Boston.

10 Car Rental

Most car rental companies have desks at Logan airport. Drivers must be aged between 21 and 75 with a valid driver's license. All agencies require a credit card or cash deposit. Collision damage waiver and liability insurances are recommended. ◈ *Alamo: 1 877 222 9075 ◈ Avis: 1 800 331 1212 ◈ Budget: 1 800 527 0700 ◈ Dollar: 1 800 800 4000 ◈ Enterprise: 1 800 736 8222 ◈ Hertz: 1 800 654 3131 ◈ Thrifty: 1 800 847 4389*

Left **Harbor Islands ferry** Center **CharlieCard** Left **Bicycling on the Esplanade**

🔟 Getting Around

Subways/Trolleys
The MBTA subway and trolley system (known collectively as the "T"), gets you close to almost anywhere in the city. Most of the lines are underground in the city center, and go partially above ground in the suburbs *(see back flap for "T" map)*. Fares are $1.70–$2 almost everywhere. ◐ *MBTA: 617 222 3200; www.mbta.com*

Buses
The MBTA bus system enlarges the transit network to cover more than 1,000 miles (1,620 km). Buses run less frequently than the "T." Make sure you have exact change ($1.50) or a CharlieCard when traveling by bus. Bus maps are available on the MBTA website or at the main office at Downtown Crossing. The Silver Line is technically a T line but it runs buses not light rail, and provides quick trips to airport terminals. Two other useful routes are Charlestown to Haymarket (No. 93) and Harvard Square to Dudley Square via Massachusetts Avenue (No. 1).

"T" Pass
A Link Pass for unlimited travel on the MBTA system, including inner harbor ferries, can be purchased for $9 for one day and $15 for seven days. Available at most subway stations.

Water Taxis & Ferries
City Water Taxi operates throughout Boston's inner harbor. Boston Harbor Cruises offers a ferry service to Provincetown from Long Wharf. The Bay State Cruise Company connects the World Trade Center with Provincetown, and the inexpensive MBTA ferry links Long Wharf to Charlestown Navy Yard *(see pp30–31)*. ◐ *City Water Taxi: 617 422 0392* ◐ *Boston Harbor Cruises: 617 227 4321* ◐ *Bay State Cruise Company: 617 748 1428*

Walking
Unlike many American cities, Downtown Boston is compact and easy to negotiate on foot.

Bicycling
Boston has many dedicated bike paths including along the Charles River and on some major streets. Cycling on highways is illegal and riding on sidewalks is discouraged and, in some places, illegal. Hubway bike sharing has 600 bicycles at 60 stations in the city (www.thehubway.com).

Finding Your Way
Use public transportation to reach neighborhood centers and explore on foot from there. If you're going farther out get the *Arrow Metro Street Atlas*.

Taxis
Taxis can be hailed on the street in the Downtown area or found at taxi stands throughout the city. Cambridge taxis can only collect in Cambridge, and Boston taxis in Boston (the only exception is at the airport). You can also call a taxi company to arrange a pick up. Rates are calculated by both mileage and time. ◐ *Boston Cab Dispatch: 617 262 2227* ◐ *Yellow Cab Cambridge: 617 547 3000*

Driving
Visitors should make sure to familiarize themselves with at least a basic understanding of US driving rules and signage. Information is available at most vehicle-rental agencies. "Rotary" traffic intersections (roundabouts) confuse even local drivers. In theory, vehicles on the rotary have right of way.

Parking
Bostonians own twice as many cars as there are spaces, so inevitably parking spaces are limited. Metered parking costs 25 cents per 12-minute period from 8am to 6pm. Garage and open-lot parking starts around $10 per hour, $40 per day. Boston Common (Charles St) and Haymarket (Congress and Sudbury sts) garages are two of the most central.

Left **Ticket office, Whale Watches** Center **Trolley tour** Right **Gondola tour**

🔟 Guided Tours & Excursions

Trolley Tours
Several city tours depart from the Visitor Information Center on Boston Common *(see p138)*, including Old Town Trolley Tours, which offers narrated sightseeing in old-fashioned trolley buses, as well as seasonal theme tours (ghosts, chocolate, etc). These trolley tours permit re-boarding all day, making them easy transit to major sites. ✈ *Old Town Trolley Tours: 617 269 7010 • www.trolleytours.com*

Water Tours
Boston Harbor Cruises depart from Long Wharf and offer harbor and lighthouse tours as well as whale-watching. Sightseeing and sunset tours of the Charles River on small cruise boats depart from Cambridgeside Galleria. The vessels of choice for wedding proposals are the two authentic Venetian gondolas moored at the Charles River Esplanade. ✈ *Boston Harbor Cruises: 617 227 4321 • www.bostonharborcruises.com* ✈ *Charles River Boat Company: 617 621 3001 • www.charlesriverboat.com* ✈ *Gondola di Venezia: 617 876 2800 or 800 979 3370 • www.bostongondolas.com*

Boston Duck Tours
Boston Duck Tours, especially popular with families *(see p60)*, use open-air amphibious vehicles that tour the streets and navigate the Charles River. ✈ *617 267 3825 • www.ducktours.com*

Boston by Foot
Enthusiastic volunteers share their love of the city on guided walks. Tour options include the Freedom Trail, Victorian Back Bay, Beacon Hill, North End, Literary Landmarks, and Boston Underfoot. ✈ *617 367 2345 • www.bostonbyfoot.com*

Park Service Ranger Tours
Boston National Historic Park rangers run tours of the Freedom Trail *(see pp8–11)*, Black Heritage Trail *(see p77)*, and Charlestown Navy Yard *(see pp30–31)*. Rangers at Frederick Law Olmsted's National Historic site run tours of portions of the Emerald Necklace, as well as tours of the office and grounds by reservation. ✈ *National Park Service: 617 242 5642* ✈ *Olmsted National Historic Site: 617 566 1689*

Charles River Park Tours
Department of Conservation and Recreation rangers lead walking tours along the river and give occasional tours of the Charles River Locks and Dam *(see p63)*. ✈ *DCR Rangers: 617 626 1250*

Movie Tours
Walk or ride a bus to iconic Boston locations featured on film and television. ✈ *On Location Tours • 800 979 3370 • www.screentours.com*

Whale Watches
The New England Aquarium operates whale watches with trained marine biologists. Ships carrying approximately 200–400 passengers make the 3.5–5 hour roundtrip to the Stellwagen Bank whale feeding grounds. Tours run from April through October. ✈ *New England Aquarium: 617 973 5281 • www.neaq.org*

Culinary Tours
Sample the colorful flavors of Boston's ethnic neighborhoods. Chinatown tours visit markets, a herbalist, and end with fresh dim sum. Boston Food Tours feature tastings, tips, and insights on the Italian food markets, restaurants, and cuisine of the North End. ✈ *Boston Food Tours: 800 979 3370 • www.bostonfoodtours.com*

Bicycle Tours
Cover ground quickly with narrated bicycle tours that include an overview of city highlights plus a few places off the tourist trail. Enjoy a ride along the Charles River, a sunset trip along the waterfront, or a fall foliage spin through the Emerald Necklace. ✈ *Urban Adventours: 617 670 0637 • www.urbanadventours.com*

Note: Horse and carriage rides operate from Quincy Market behind South Market building (late May–mid-Oct; $30 for two people)

Left **Information kiosk, Boston Common** Right **Magazine stand**

TOP10 Useful Information

1 Information Kiosks

The Boston Convention and Visitors Bureau (BCVB) operates two information centers with multilingual counselors and free information. One is on the northeastern edge of Boston Common (see pp14–15), the other on the main floor of the Prudential Center. There's also an information kiosk at Harvard Square.
Ⓢ *BCVB: 1 888 733 2678*

2 Websites

For extensive information on Boston, including promotional rates at hotels and a detailed calendar of events, check the BCVB website (www.bostonusa.com). The Cambridge Office of Tourism maintains a smaller site (www.cambridge-usa.org). For foodies, Boston Chefs Collaborative site (www.bostonchefs.com) displays the current menus of many Boston restaurants.

3 Events Listings

The Boston Globe's (www.boston.com/thingstodo) calendar section is the leading source of information about upcoming events. Similar listings appear in the *Boston Phoenix* (www.thephoenix.com), which focuses on the club and bar scene. Boston Citysearch (www.boston.citysearch.com) posts entertainment listings and restaurant reviews.

4 Radio & TV

Boston's competitive media market includes all the US network broadcasters: CBS (channel 4), ABC (channel 5), NBC (channel 7), Fox (channel 25), and UPN (channel 56). All five stations have strong local news and weather programs. New England Cable News provides non-stop regional news coverage. Channel 2 is a leading program producer for the national public broadcasting system (PBS). Radio station WBUR (90.9 FM) originates the humorous "Car Talk" which muses on life and love while dispensing auto repair advice. Other popular Boston stations include WFNX (101.7 FM) for rock music and WCRB (99.5 FM) for classical.

5 Opening Hours

Most stores and attractions are open daily, although many museums close on Mondays. Banks close on weekends; post offices close on Sundays. Hours and days of opening may become abbreviated during winter periods – check with venues.

6 Tipping

Plan to tip for most services: 15–20 per cent to waitstaff; $1 per bag for porters; $2 to valet parking attendants; about 50 cents–$1 per drink to bartenders, and 10 per cent plus the change up to the next dollar for taxi drivers.

7 Smoking

Smoking is prohibited in most public indoor spaces. Check for no-smoking signs before lighting up. Massachusetts has very high tobacco prices and requires photo ID proving age of 18 or older to purchase cigarettes.

8 Drinking

You must be 21 or over to buy alcohol and the law requires bartenders or store clerks to check photo ID if in doubt.

9 Consulates

While Boston-based consulates cannot intervene in legal matters with local authorities they can provide limited services and referrals for visiting nationals.
Ⓢ *Canadian: 3 Copley Pl • 617 247 5100* Ⓢ *Great Britain and Northern Ireland: 1 Broadway, Cambridge • 617 245 4500* Ⓢ *Ireland: 535 Boylston St • 617 267 9330*

10 Public Holidays

New Year's Day (Jan 1); Martin Luther King, Jr. Day (3rd Mon in Jan); Presidents' Day (3rd Mon in Feb); Evacuation Day (Mar 17); Patriots' Day (3rd Mon in Apr); Memorial Day (Last Mon in May); Independence Day (Jul 4); Labor Day (1st Mon in Sep); Columbus Day (2nd Mon in Oct); Veterans' Day (Nov 11); Thanksgiving (4th Thu in Nov); Christmas Day (Dec 25).

 Note: For lost property call Boston Police Department Lost Property Office 8am–4pm at 617 343 4200

Left **Disabled sign** Center **Local taxi** Right **A Huntington Theatre production**

🔟 Boston for Special Needs

1 Sources of Information

VSA Arts publishes *Access Expressed!*, a $20 guide to accessibility at arts venues, public buildings, and some hotels and restaurants in Boston and New England; call to request a copy. VSA Arts' principal website (*www.vsamass. org*) lists a calendar of accessible arts events. The New England Index website (*www.disability-info.org*) gives hundreds of sources of aid for the disabled. ✆ *VSA Arts: 617 350 7713 • TTY: 617 350 6536*

2 Wheelchair Access

All facilities built or renovated since 1987 are legally required to provide wheelchair accessible entrances and restrooms. Most attractions are wheelchair accessible. Anticipate problems in historic buildings and older B&Bs and restaurants by calling ahead.

3 Aids for the Hearing Impaired

The following venues offer listening aids for the hearing impaired. Wheelock Family Theatre and Huntington Theatre also offer performances signed in ASL (American sign language). ✆ *Cutler Majestic Theater: 617 824 8000* ✆ *Jordan Hall: 617 585 1260* ✆ *Wheelock Family Theater: 617 879 2300 • TTY 617 879 2150*

✆ *Huntington Theatre Company: 617 266 0800*

4 Aids for the Visually Impaired

Guide dogs are permitted in all establishments. Most busy road intersections have audio signals to indicate safe crossing times. The Wheelock and the Huntington theaters (*see above*) offer audio descriptions of some performances. The New England Aquarium (*see pp32–3*), Museum of Science (*see p60*), and Museum of Fine Arts (*see pp22–5*) have tactile displays for the visually impaired.

5 Taxis

The following taxi companies will send wheelchair accessible vehicles on request. ✆ *Boston Cab: 617 536 5010* ✆ *Checker Cab – Cambridge: 800 616 1220* ✆ *Town Taxi: 617 536 5000*

6 Public Transit

Most buses, subways, commuter rail lines, and ferries are at least partially accessible for wheelchair users. ✆ *MBTA Office for Transportation Access (OTA): 617 222 5123 • TTY: 617 222 5415*

7 Restrooms

Visitors' centers, museums, and galleries have public restrooms with disabled and baby-changing facilities. There are a few high-tech public toilet kiosks along parts of the Freedom Trail (*see pp8–11*).

8 Children's Needs

Some hotels permit children under a certain age to stay in their parents' room for free, and some offer family rates. The concierges at most larger downtown hotels can arrange babysitting. Short-term babysitting can also be arranged through Parents-in-a-Pinch. For child-oriented services and entertainment, pick up a free *Parents Paper* at libraries and grocery stores. ✆ *Parents-in-a-Pinch: 617 739 5437 • www.parentsinapinch.com • http://boston.parenthood.com*

9 Legal Assistance

US citizens in need of legal assistance should contact the Boston Bar Association's lawyer referral service; non-US citizens should telephone their consulate for legal assistance (check Blue Pages), or their embassy in Washington, D.C. ✆ *Legal Advocacy & Resource Center: 617 742 0625*

10 Special Tours

The Alternative Leisure Company arranges excursions for persons with special needs, including physical disabilities. Outdoor Exploration organizes active sports outings for the physically and developmentally challenged. ✆ *Alternative Leisure Company: 1 781 275 0023 • www.alctrips.com* ✆ *Outdoor Exploration: 1 781 395 4999 • www.outdoorexp.org*

Share your travel recommendations on traveldk.com

Left **Post office** Center **Boston phone card** Right **Public telephones**

🔟 Banking & Communications

1 Banking Hours
Most banks are open Monday to Friday from 9am to 2pm or later, and on Saturdays from 9am to noon or 1pm. Banks close on Sundays and holidays.

2 Currency Exchange
Currency exchange is available at main branches of large banks, which are generally open weekdays from 9am to 5pm (passport required). Travelex has a booth at 745 Boylston St. ⊛ www.travelex.com

3 Travelers' Checks
Dollar-denominated travelers' checks issued by American Express or Thomas Cook are widely accepted; personal checks from foreign banks are not. American Express offices will cash checks for their cardholders.
⊛ *American Express Travel Service: 31 St. James Ave • 125 High St • 39 JFK St, Cambridge*

4 ATMs
ATMs (cash machines) are usually found near bank entrances. Widely accepted cards include Cirrus, Plus, NYCE, and Visa and MasterCard credit cards. Most ATMs levy a withdrawal fee for cards not affiliated to that bank. It's often cheaper to withdraw money using a debit card.

5 Credit Cards
American Express, Visa, MasterCard, Diners Club, and Discover are widely accepted. Credit cards are safer than carrying cash and may offer benefits such as insurance and favorable exchange rates. They are essential to reserve a hotel room or book a rental car.

6 Internet Access
Many hotels and B&Bs offer Internet access for guests with their own computers. High-speed access usually requires an Ethernet or Wi-Fi card, while dial-up connections require an RJ-11 connector. Free wireless networks can usually be found in the big-name coffee shops and bookstores, and in well-known burger chains.

7 Telephones
Most accept coins as well as phone cards. Prepaid phone cards (available at gas stations, convenience stores, and newsstands) are the least expensive way to call long distance. Local calls cost $0.50–1 for three minutes from pay phones but are free from private land lines. Directory inquiries are free from public phones. Note, you always need to dial the 617 within Boston. Dial a 1 for other US codes. To dial abroad, key 011 followed by the country code and the city code (omitting any initial 0). Try Roberts Rent-a-Phone if you want to hire a cell phone. ⊛ *Roberts Rent-a-Phone: 800 964 2468*

8 Sending Mail
Most Boston-area post offices are open from 8am to 6pm Monday to Friday, and Saturday from 8am to noon. The main General Post Office is open 6am to midnight. Letters and parcels weighing less than 13 oz (370 g) can be put in any blue mailbox. ⊛ *General Post Office: 25 Dorchester Ave • Map Q5 • 617 654 5302 • For branch locations: 1 800 725 2161*

9 Express & Courier Delivery
The US Postal Service Express Mail next-day delivery service starts at $18.95 for up to 8 oz (256 g); global 2–3 day delivery costs from $29.25. Next-day delivery is also available from Federal Express and United Parcel Service.
⊛ *Federal Express: 1 800 247 4747* ⊛ *United Parcel Service: 1 800 742 5877*

10 Boston Newspapers
The *Boston Globe* is the dominant newspaper; the tabloid *Boston Herald* is widely available as well. Newsstands also carry *USA Today*, *The New York Times*, and *The Wall Street Journal*. For a good selection of non-Boston newspapers try Out of Town News or other newsstands in and around the Harvard area. ⊛ *Out of Town News: 0 Harvard Sq, Cambridge • 617 354 7777*

Note: The Yellow Pages telephone directory lists numbers organized by service. You can look them up online at www.superpages.com

Streetsmart

Left **Fire engine** Center **Local policeman** Right **Pedestrian crossing sign**

TOP 10 Security & Health

1 Preventing Theft
Keep camera bags, backpacks, and purses on your person. Before you leave home, make photocopies of important documents, including your passport and visa, and keep them with you, separate from the originals Also make a note of your credit card numbers (and the phone number to call if they are stolen).

2 Crossing the Street
Cross at marked cross walks, obeying the "walk" signal lights. Intersections without "walk" signals indicate when pedestrians should cross the road with a combined red-and-amber signal.

3 Avoiding Muggers
Muggings are rare in Boston. Avoid poorly lit and deserted areas, like Boston Common, at night, especially if alone. Know where you are going and walk purposefully. Study your map before leaving, rather than on the street Keep only small amounts of cash in your pockets and if confronted by a mugger, give up your money promptly.

4 Hotel Room Safety
When checking in, learn the fire escape route from your room. Keep valuables in your hotel safe, otherwise hotels will not guarantee their security. Use the peephole or chain to confirm the identity of anyone who knocks at your door before letting them in.

5 Telephone Hotlines
For police, fire, or ambulance, dial 911. Stay on the line even if you are unable to speak so the emergency locator system can track you. Emergency calls are free.

6 Hospitals
The Boston area has both city-run (public) and private hospitals. Public facilities, listed in the phone book Blue Pages, can be overcrowded but are often less expensive. Private hospitals, listed in the Yellow Pages, rank among some of the world's best and charge accordingly.

7 Dental Emergencies
The Massachusetts Dental Society can offer referrals to private dentists for emergency work. Tufts Dental School also runs an emergency dental clinic in Chinatown.
◈ *Massachusetts Dental Society • 1 800 342 8747 • www.massdental.org*
◈ *Tufts Dental School, 1 Kneeland St • 617 636 6828*

8 Medical Emergencies
Your medical insurer should cover all costs, but in order to avoid paying your medical bill and then have money reimbursed it is always best to contact your insurance company before seeking treatment. You will then be directed to a hospital that will deal directly with your insurer. If you need an ambulance, call 911. The Massachusetts General Hospital is centrally located for emergencies. For referrals, contact Massachusetts Medical Society. ◈ *Massachusetts General Hospital: 55 Fruit St • Map N2 • 617 726 2000* ◈ *Massachusetts Medical Society • 781 893 4610 or 1 800 322 2303*

9 Pharmacies
Bring copies of prescriptions for medications you are taking. Pharmacies abound, ask your hotel for the nearest one.
◈ *CVS Pharmacy: 35 White St, Cambridge • 617 876 5519 • Open 24 hrs*
◈ *CVS Pharmacy: 155 Charles St • 617 523 1028 • Open 24 hours, pharmacy open 8am–8pm Mon–Sat, 10am–8pm Sun*

10 Insect-borne Diseases
Three insect-borne infectious diseases (Lyme disease, eastern equine encephalitis, and West Nile virus) have been reported in rural areas of eastern Massachusetts. Exposure within metropolitan Boston is extremely unlikely. If worried, use mosquito repellent and keep arms, legs, and ankles covered.

 Note: *The Blue Pages phone directory lists numbers for government agencies in alphabetical order by city, state, and federal*

Streetsmart

Left **BosTix kiosk** Center **Discount tickets** Right **Free Hatch Shell concert, The Esplanade**

TOP 10 Boston on a Budget

1 Free Admission Times
Many Boston museums offer free admission. Entry to the Museum of Fine Arts is by donation on Wednesday after 4pm. The Institute of Contemporary Art is free to visit on Thursday after 5pm. The Boston Children's Museum charges $1 on Friday evenings. The Isabella Stewart Gardner Museum is free on a visitor's birthday.

2 Free Summer Venues
Hatch Shell (see p52) stages concerts during the summer as well as several of the Boston Pops concerts during the week around July 4 (see p54). On Friday evenings, Hatch Shell shows big-screen family films. Check Boston Globe "Calendar" (see p138) for specifics, as well as for details on concerts on City Hall Plaza and Copley Square. The Commonwealth Shakespeare Company performs on Boston Common during July and August. ✪ Concert hotline: 617 727 1300, ext. 555 ✪ Commonwealth Shakespeare: 617 426 0863 www.commshakes.org

3 Gallery Hopping
College and university art galleries mount some of the city's most provocative exhibitions with free admission.

4 Bargain Tickets
BosTix kiosks sell half-price tickets to most non-commercial arts events and to some commercial productions from 10am on the day of performance (11am Sun). Purchases must be made in person. ✪ Faneuil Hall Marketplace & Copley Sq • 617 262 8632 • www. bostix.com • Open 10am–6pm Mon–Sat, 11am–4pm Sun

5 Symphony Savings
Last-minute tickets for Boston Symphony Orchestra performances at the Symphony Hall (see p52) on Tuesday, Thursday, and Friday evenings and Friday afternoons are 50–85 percent of the usual cost. General admission to open rehearsals is also available at a reduced price. ✪ Symphony Hall, 301 Massachusetts Ave • 617 266 1492

6 Theater Deals
Some of Boston's largest theaters offer ticket bargains. The Huntington Theatre has $25 tickets for those under 35 years of age; and the American Repertory Theatre usually sells discounted day-of-show tickets for students. ✪ Huntington Theatre: 617 266 0800 ✪ American Repertory Theatre: 617 547 8300

7 Music Schools
Boston's music schools present ambitious performance seasons of students, faculty, and guest artists. Berklee Performance Center (see p53) at the Berklee School of Music has more than 100 shows per year (shows by students and faculty cost less than $10), as does The New England Conservatory (see p52), which holds free performances at Jordan Hall. ✪ Berklee Performance Center: 617 266 7455 ✪ Jordan Hall: 617 585 1260

8 Public Transit Passes
Cut transportation costs with a Link Pass allowing unlimited travel on subways, buses, and ferries for one or seven days (see p136).

9 City Pass
A City Pass ($46) gives access to the Prudential Skywalk, Museum of Fine Arts, Museum of Science, New England Aquarium, and Harvard's Natural History Museum or Old State House. Valid for nine days, it's available at Visitor Information Centers and saves 50 percent on admission charges.

10 Special Discounts
Student and senior citizen discounts are often available with appropriate identification. Members of the American Automobile Association (AAA) or affiliated auto clubs of other countries should inquire about discounts at hotels, motels, and attractions.

  Note: For more information on Boston event listings, which include free/reduced price performances See p138

Left **Line, USS Constitution** Center **Cheers sign** Right **Tow truck**

🔟 Things to Avoid

1 Tourist Traps
Avoid any eating or drinking establishment that claims to have been around since colonial days. Also attractions that claim a close affiliation with TV series (such as *Cheers*) have usually lost their original charm.

2 Lines & Crowds
A Link Pass (see p136) lets you bypass the "T" ticket machine. Avoid traveling from 8 to 9:30am and 4 to 6:30pm to beat the crowds. The biggest bottlenecks for entrance into most performance venues are at the "will-call" window, where you pick up pre-booked tickets, and the box office.

3 Taking the Wrong "T"
To avoid going the wrong direction on the subway, remember that all trains headed toward Downtown Crossing, Park Street, or State "T" stations are "inbound." All trains head away are "outbound." Platforms for outbound and inbound trains often have different entrances. Be especially careful on the green line, which branches into four separate lines. The red line also branches into two south of the city. Check the final destination of the train you want against the MBTA map. Signs on the front and side of the train always list its final destination.

4 Parking Fines & Towing
You are likely to be towed if you park illegally in a tow zone, which will be signposted. In addition to towing fees, you'll also pay a large fine before your car is released. You will also get a ticket for parking at an expired meter or in a resident-only zone. It's impossible to escape payment. Rental companies will charge your credit card, and if it's your own car, your home state will not renew your license or registration until you pay.

5 Hotel Extras
Many hotels greatly inflate the cost of calls. Some may charge as much as $2 for a local call or a toll-free call. Save money by purchasing a prepaid phone card and using the lobby pay phone. Hotel breakfasts, unless explicitly included in the room rate, are also often outrageously high-priced. Most cafés will fill you to overflowing for less than $10.

6 Pickpockets
Boston has its share of pickpockets, who often work in pairs, with one creating a diversion while the other relieves you of your wallet. Be careful in crowds and when boarding or leaving buses and subway trains. Consider using a hidden travel wallet for the bulk of your funds.

7 Ticket Scalpers
Anti-scalping (touting) laws are hard to enforce. Scalpers ply their trade openly outside sports venues and theaters. Buyer beware: ticket prices are often highly inflated over face value and the tickets may be fake.

8 Beggars
Boston has a large population of homeless people, many of whom beg on the street. One way to help the homeless is by purchasing a copy of *Spare Change*, the weekly newspaper produced and edited by the homeless.

9 Traffic Jams
Traffic jams are at their worst from 8 to 10am, and 4 to 6pm on weekdays. Highway traffic around Boston is very heavy on Fridays from noon to 7pm and on Sundays from 4 to 8pm. There are always some delays along the harbor and river roads, and on streets around Beacon Hill and Boston Common.

10 Jaywalking
The laws against jaywalking are rarely enforced by police, but crossing outside marked crosswalks is dangerous. Boston drivers have hair-trigger reflexes when they see an opening to accelerate, and much slower reflexes when it's time to stop.

Left **Prudential Center shopping mall** Center **Sign, Brattle Bookshop** Right **Fresh produce**

🔟 Shopping Tips

1 Store Hours
Most stores open from 10am to 6pm Monday through Saturday (usually later on Thursday) and noon to 5 or 6pm on Sunday. Department stores often stay open a little later. Widely observed retail holidays are Christmas day, January 1, July 4, and Thanksgiving (4th Thursday in November).

2 Taxes
State sales tax of 6.25 percent is added to all purchases, except clothing and groceries. Clothing costing $175 or more, however, is subject to a 6.25 percent luxury tax.

3 Sales Periods
Look for end-of-season savings on merchandise. Expect sales during the Christmas shopping season, but greater discounts in January.

4 Department Stores
Boston's most traditional department store, Macy's (see p57), is located at Downtown Crossing. In Back Bay, Lord and Taylor is known for classic clothing, Saks Fifth Avenue for following fashion trends, and Neiman Marcus for luxury items. 🛇 Macy's: 450 Washington St • Map P4 🛇 Lord & Taylor: 760 Boylston St • Map L5 🛇 Saks Fifth Avenue: Prudential Center, 800 Boylston St • Map K6 🛇 Neiman Marcus: 5 Copley Pl • Map L5

5 Shopping Malls
Boston's shopping malls are ideal for a rainy day. In Back Bay, a pedestrian walkway joins upscale Copley Place to the completely revitalized Prudential Center (see p82). Cambridgeside Galleria has many mid-priced shops. 🛇 Copley Place: 100 Huntington Ave • Map L5 🛇 Prudential Center: 800 Boylston St • Map K6 🛇 Cambridgeside Galleria: 100 Cambridgeside Pl • Map F2

6 Discount Outlets
Wrentham Village Premium Outlets, a mall with 170 shops carrying low-priced top-name brands in clothing and housewares, is a 45-minute drive southwest from Boston. Daily bus service ($36) includes hotel pickup. 🛇 Brush Hill Tours: 1 781 986 6100

7 Food & Drink
For unusual gifts, and a taste of New England at home, James Hook & Co will airship live lobsters. For farmhouse cheeses, it's worth visiting Formaggio Kitchen and South End Formaggio. 🛇 Formaggio Kitchen: 244 Huron Ave, Cambridge 🛇 James Hook & Co: 15 Northern Ave • Map R4 🛇 South End Formaggio: 268 Shawmut Ave • Map F6

8 Music & Books
Newbury Comics in Back Bay has a large CD collection. Try Skippy White's for R&B and gospel; Orpheus for classical and jazz; and Franklin's CD for Latin music. Harvard Square (see p57) has one of the largest bookstore concentrations in the country but collectors of rare books should head to Brattle Book Shop near Downtown Crossing. 🛇 Brattle Book Shop: 9 West St • Map C2 🛇 Franklin's CD: 314 Centre St, Jamaica Plain 🛇 Orpheus: 362 Commonwealth Ave • Map J5 🛇 Skippy White's: 1971 Columbus Ave, Roxbury 🛇 Newbury Comics: 332 Newbury St • Map L5

9 Size Conversions
Size conversions between US, UK, and European countries are complicated, and differ for men's and women's clothing and shoes. The website www.onlineconversion.com/clothing.htm will help.

10 Fine Crafts
Boston is a wonderfully rich market for artisan jewelry, accessories, and all kinds of other crafts. Mobilia is the leading gallery for an international selection of these items. The venerable Society of Arts and Crafts (see p21) sells an extensive range of work by local and emerging US artists. 🛇 Mobilia: 358 Huron Ave, Cambridge • Society of Arts & Crafts: 175 Newbury St • Map L5

Left **Bostonians dining out** Center **Seafood, Grill 23** Right **Apartment, B&B Agency of Boston**

TOP 10 Accommodation & Dining Tips

1 Location & Booking

Hotels and inns outside the city center charge the lowest prices. Those in central Boston close to principal tourist attractions, namely Back Bay, Beacon Hill, Downtown, and the Financial District, charge higher prices. The Boston CVB offers a comprehensive list but does not provide a walk-in service. For bed-and-breakfast properties, contact Host Homes of Boston. In case the property does not meet expectations, prepay only the first night. ◈ Boston CVB: www.bostonusa.com ◈ Host Homes of Boston: 617 244 1308 • www. hosthomesofboston.com

2 Room & Bed Sizes

Travelers accustomed to large motel rooms may be surprised by the small dimensions of some rooms in older Boston hotels. European-style twin-bedded rooms are uncommon; most have two double beds or one queen- or king-size bed.

3 Efficiency Units

Significant savings on breakfasts, snacks, and light meals can be realized in "efficiency" (self catering) rooms or apartments. Booking agencies, such as the B&B Agency of Boston, can arrange efficiencies in convenient locations. ◈ B&B Agency of Boston: 617 720 3540,

1 800 248 9262 • www. boston-bnbagency.com

4 Taxes

Restaurant bills incur 7 percent sales tax. Hotel tax in the Boston area is 14.45 percent. Room rates are usually quoted without tax.

5 Meal Times

Restaurants start serving breakfast as early as 5:30am and usually continue until 10am. Lunch is usually available from 11:30am to 2pm. Tea falls between 4 and 6pm. Some restaurants begin serving dinner around 5:30pm and few restaurants serve meals after 10pm. Many restaurants, especially in the South End, have weekend brunch from late morning into early afternoon.

6 Reservations

Reservations are usually recommended. For Boston's Top 10 Restaurants (see pp40–41), try to book two weeks ahead. Alternatively, call at dinner time to see if there are no-shows or cancelations. Some very popular restaurants do not accept reservations, assuming diners will simply stand and wait.

7 Etiquette

Be punctual for reservations. Many restaurants, both fancy and casual, now ban cellphones so it's best to switch yours off when dining.

8 Cuisine Styles

The best Boston chefs borrow liberally from cuisines all over the world, creating a complex style often called "New American". This new cuisine employs local produce and is lighter than traditional American cooking. The strongest influence on Boston cooking is Mediterranean fare of France and Italy, with a growing interest in Spanish, Portuguese, and North African traditions. Most fine-dining restaurants offer at least one vegetarian main dish.

9 Portions

At most Boston restaurants it is usual to expect vast portions. One portion will often suffice for two people, and sharing can be a good way to save money. It is also acceptable to ask for a "doggie bag" to take home any leftovers.

10 Boston Seafood

Boston remains a major fishing port and so inevitably delicious fresh seafood is plentiful. Top choice is usually the sweet-tasting, large-clawed American lobster. In the Boston area, young haddock or cod is often called "scrod". Bluefish is a strong-flavored, oily fish belonging to the mackerel/tuna family. A quahog is a large clam, and local oysters are known as American bluepoints.

 Note: Camping is available on Grape, Bumpkin, Peddocks, and Lovell islands **See pp66–7**

Left **Four Seasons** Right **Bar, XV Beacon**

Top 10 Luxury Hotels

1 Ritz-Carlton Boston Common

Post-modernism triumphs in this classy hotel on the upper levels of the tallest building overlooking the Common. The rooms are the height of contemporary elegance. Guests can use the fitness center for a nominal charge. There is an upscale cinema a few floors down. 🅢 *10 Avery St, 02111 • Map N4 • 617 574 7100 • www. ritz-carlton.com • $$$$$*

2 Four Seasons

Rock stars and visiting dignitaries often select the low-key luxury of this modern hotel situated on the edge of the Theater District. The lobby-level Bristol Lounge is a favorite spot for striking business deals, and the indoor pool is an added bonus. 🅢 *200 Boylston St, 02116 • Map N4 • 617 338 4400 • www.fourseasons. com • $$$$$*

3 Langham, Boston

The extremely posh Langham occupies a jewel of an Art Nouveau building, the former Federal Reserve bank in the heart of the Financial District. Spacious rooms feature modernized Second Empire decor with rich brocades. 🅢 *250 Franklin St, 02110 • Map Q3 • 617 451 1900 • www.langham boston.com • $$$$*

4 Taj Boston

The 1927 "original" Boston Ritz on the edge of the Common had a thorough restoration in 2002 to revive its old-fashioned glory. This grande dame epitomizes opulence, decorum, and "old Boston" style. The lobby bar is legendary. 🅢 *15 Arlington St, 02116 • Map M4 • 617 536 5700 • www.tajhotels.com • $$$$*

5 XV Beacon

The design-conscious decor and extraordinary attention to detail makes this chic but cozy boutique hotel in Beacon Hill a favorite with business execs. With just 60 rooms, all with high-tech extras, it is the most masculine of Boston's modern hotels. 🅢 *15 Beacon St, 02108 • Map P3 • 617 670 1500 • www.xvbeacon.com • $$$$*

6 Liberty Hotel

Dramatic design has transformed the historic Charles Street Jail into an elegant boutique hotel with a soaring lobby. Basketball and hockey teams stay here, as TD Garden is nearby. 🅢 *215 Charles St, 02114 • Map F3 • 617 224 4000 • www.liberty hotel.com • $$$$$*

7 Eliot

Back Bay grace characterizes this late 19th-century landmark hotel. Visiting musicians and baseball teams alike enjoy the spacious suites. Clio *(see p89)*, the ground-floor restaurant, is one of Boston's best and provides room service for guests. 🅢 *370 Commonwealth Ave, 02215 • Map J5 • 617 267 1607 • www.eliothotel.com • $$$$*

8 Mandarin Oriental

Situated in the heart of Back Bay, the Mandarin Oriental has some of the city's largest luxury rooms. The rooms come fitted with designer linens, large bathtubs, and state-of-the-art electronics. Many guests stay on site to enjoy the full-service spa. 🅢 *776 Boylston St, 2199 • Map K6 • 866 526 6567 or 617 535 8888 • www.mandarinoriental. com • $$$$$*

9 Boston Harbor

To enjoy one of the most beautiful locations in the city to the full, request a room with a harbor view and private balcony. There's no need to go anywhere else with restaurants, fitness center, and spa all on site. 🅢 *70 Rowes Wharf, 02110 • Map R3 • 617 439 7000 • www.bhh.com • $$$$*

10 Millennium Bostonian

Rooms run the gamut from tiny to palatial in this elegant and swanky oasis close to bustling Faneuil Hall Marketplace *(see pp12–13)*. There is an excellent on-site fitness center. 🅢 *Faneuil Hall Marketplace, 02109 • Map Q2 • 617 523 3600 • www.millennium hotels.com • $$$$*

Note: *Unless otherwise stated, all hotels accept credit cards and have en-suite bathrooms and air conditioning*

Price Categories

For a standard, double room per night (with breakfast if included), taxes, and extra charges.

$	under $150
$$	$150–$250
$$$	$250–$350
$$$$	$350–$450
$$$$$	over $450

Left **Fairmont Battery Wharf**

TOP 10 Deluxe Hotels

1 Charles

Extra touches, such as handmade quilts hanging on the walls, personalize the surprisingly comfortable rooms at this modern hotel on the edge of Harvard Square. There's an indoor pool, an outstanding jazz club, Reggatabar *(see p47)*, and a leading Boston restaurant, Rialto *(see p40)*. ✪ *1 Bennett St, Cambridge, 02138 • Map B2 • 617 864 1200 • www.charleshotel.com • $$$*

2 Ames Hotel

An elegant contemporary hotel, housed in a landmark building in the heart of downtown Boston, the Ames often has excellent weekend rates because it is mainly a business hotel. Suites have original fireplaces and windows with dramatic Romanesque arches. The minimalist room design tends towards the soothing rather than the stark ✪ *1 Court St, 02108 • Map G3 • 617 979 8100 • www.ameshotel.com • $$$$*

3 Royal Sonesta

An outstanding art collection and a striking riverside location make the Sonesta a top choice for aesthetes. Bargain summer family packages often available. Excellent restaurant. ✪ *5 Cambridge Pkwy, Cambridge, 02142 • Map F2 • 617 806 4200 • www.sonesta.com • $$$$*

4 Seaport

Connected by a walkway to the World Trade Center, the Seaport was one of the first to pioneer the new waterfront district. The price is right for large and comfortable rooms and the pool is a bonus. Regular shuttles to downtown help ease the isolation. ✪ *1 Seaport Lane, 02210 • 617 385 4000 • www.seaporthotel.com • $$$*

5 Inn at Harvard

The clubby feel of this comfortable, modern, atrium-style hotel fits its Harvard association perfectly. The university often takes many of the 111 rooms for visiting academics, so the hotel can get very busy. ✪ *1201 Massachusetts Ave, Cambridge, 02138 • Map B1 • 617 491 2222 • www.theinnatharvard.com • $$$*

6 Hotel Marlowe

Opened in 2002, this sleek hotel creates a self-contained world of comfort with Internet access, evening wine receptions, and fitness center. Check the website for last-minute deals. ✪ *25 Edwin H. Land Blvd, Cambridge, 02141 • Map F2 • 617 868 8000 • www.hotelmarlowe.com • $$$$*

7 Colonnade

Frequently used by upscale bus groups, the Colonnade has some of the largest and most comfortable rooms in Back Bay, as well as the city's only outdoor rooftop pool. Very family-friendly. ✪ *120 Huntington Ave, 02116 • Map K6 • 617 424 7000 • www.colonnadehotel.com • $$$*

8 Marriott Long Wharf

The hotel's waterfront location means most of the bright, spacious rooms have superb harbor or city views. Waterline, the casual bar-restaurant, is the perfect spot for an evening cocktail. ✪ *296 State St, 02109 • Map R2 • 617 227 0800 • www.marriottlongwharf.com • $$$$*

9 Fairmont Battery Wharf

Situated at the edge of the North End, this luxurious hotel commands the mouth of Boston Harbor. Guests benefit from a well-equipped fitness center and a luxury spa. ✪ *3 Battery Wharf, 02109 • Map H2 • 617 994 9000 • www.fairmont.com • $$$$*

10 Nine Zero

Nine Zero marries sleek and shiny steel, chrome, and glass with warm woods and designer furniture to achieve a contemporary look with a soft edge. Its location, on the Downtown Crossing corner of Boston Common, is very convenient. ✪ *90 Tremont St, 02108 • Map G3–G4 • 617 722 5800 • www.ninezerohotel.com • $$$*

Left **Charles Street Inn** Center **Fairmont Copley Plaza** Right **Gryphon House**

TOP 10 Hip/Historic Stays

1 Fairmont Copley Plaza

This sister hotel of New York's Plaza has been a Copley Square landmark since 1912. Public areas are opulent, rooms are small but comfy, and suites are truly grand. Richard Burton and Liz Taylor are among the stars who have stayed here. ◐ 138 St James Ave, 02116 • Map L5 • 617 267 5300 • www.fairmont.com • $$$$

2 W Hotel

Seemingly designed as much for the architectural press as for the traveler, this W appeals equally to design mavens, and to visitors who enjoy the location in the Theater District at the edge of Back Bay. A Bliss Spa is in the hotel. ◐ 100 Stuart St, 02116 • Map G5 • 617 261 8700 • www.starwoodhotels.com • $$$$

3 Hotel InterContinental

This chic waterfront hotel at the edge of Fort Point Channel combines sophisticated architecture with luxurious decor of rich furnishings and textiles. Sumptuous bathrooms include a soaking tub as well as shower. ◐ 510 Atlantic Ave, 02110 • Map H4 • 617 747 1000 • www.intercontinental boston.com • $$$

4 Charles Street Inn

Constructed in 1860 as a showpiece for new homes in the area, this Beacon Hill hideaway boasts Victorian features, such as carved marble fireplaces, with European furnishings. Modern touches include Internet access and whirlpool tubs. ◐ 94 Charles St, 02114 • Map M3 • 617 314 8900 • www.charlesstreet inn.com • $$$$

5 Beacon Hill Hotel & Bistro

This townhouse hotel is mere steps from Boston Common (see p14–15). The rooms are mostly small but Euro-chic, and there's a first-floor bistro that serves breakfast (included in rates). There's even a private roofdeck for guests. ◐ 25 Charles St, 02114 • Map N3 • 617 723 7575 • www.beaconhill hotel.com • $$$

6 Gryphon House

This brownstone townhouse, c.1895, boasts eight huge, elegant rooms with fireplaces, wet bars, CD-players, and high-speed Internet access. A quiet spot, it is equally convenient for Back Bay or the Fenway. ◐ 9 Bay State Rd, 02215 • Map D5 • 617 375 9003 • www.gryphonhouseboston.com • No DA • $$

7 Hotel Commonwealth

This suave 150-room hotel has all the high-tech essentials but with the architecture and decor of France's Second Empire. ◐ 500 Commonwealth Ave, 02215 • Map D5 • 617 933 5000 • www.hotel commonwealth.com • $$$

8 Hotel Veritas

This luxury four-story boutique hotel near Harvard University is ideally situated for families visiting students. Combining luxury with convenience, rooms are intimate and contemporary, while bathrooms have marble finishes. A cozy lounge in the lobby serves cocktails. ◐ 1 Remington St, 02138 • Map C2 • 617 520 5000 • www.thehotelveritas.com • $$$

9 Boston Park Plaza

With 941 rooms on 15 floors, the 1927 Park Plaza is Boston's largest historic hotel. Restoration has thankfully put some glamour back. Popular with business travelers, convention goers, and tour packagers, it is convenient for Back Bay and the Theater District. ◐ 64 Arlington St, 02116 • Map M5 • 617 426 2000 • www.bostonparkplaza.com • $$

10 The Back Bay Hotel

This Irish boutique hotel in the handsome limestone, former Boston police headquarters offers deluxe comfort and services in a convenient corner of South End. ◐ 350 Stuart St, 02116 • Map F5 • 617 266 7200 • www.doylecollection.com • $$$$

 Note: Unless otherwise stated, all hotels accept credit cards and have en-suite bathrooms and air conditioning

Price Categories

For a standard, double room per night (with breakfast if included), taxes, and extra charges.

$	under $150
$$	$150–$250
$$$	$250–$350
$$$$	$350–$450
$$$$$	over $450

Left **Charlesmark**

🔟 Mid-Range Hotels

1 Harborside Inn
This modest boutique hotel is in an old (1858) spice warehouse. Guest rooms have wood floors, exposed brick walls, oriental rugs, and traditional furnishings. ◈ *185 State St, 02109 • Map Q3 • 617 723 7500, 888 723 7565 • www.harborsideinnboston.com • $$*

2 Westin Boston Waterfront
Connected to the Boston Convention & Exhibition Center, with excellent conference facilities, this huge property serves business travelers well. A complimentary shuttle provides transport to nearby attractions and an on-site gym affords the opportunity for a workout. ◈ *425 Summer St, 02210 • Map P4 • 617 532 4600 • www.starwood hotels.com • $$$*

3 Kendall
An artist-architect couple transformed this century-old Cambridge firehouse into a boutique hotel. The 77 rooms are decorated with firehouse memorabilia and antiques. ◈ *350 Main St, Cambridge, 02142 • Map E3 • 617 577 1300 • www.kendallhotel.com • $$*

4 Days Hotel
Barely within the city limits, the 117-room Days Hotel offers clean and basic accommodation. Located on the Charles River, some rooms have attractive water views, and it's only a 15-minute or so walk into Harvard Square. ◈ *1234 Soldiers Field Rd, 02135 • Map B2 • 617 254 1234 • www.days hotelboston.com • $$*

5 Courtyard Boston Cambridge
Large desks and great views are highlights of this older riverfront hotel. Amenities include a fitness center and an indoor pool. The location isn't ideal unless you have a car. ◈ *777 Memorial Dr, Cambridge, 02139 • Map B3 • 617 492 7777 • www.marriott.com • $$$*

6 Sheraton Commander
Harvard Square's original (1927) hotel emerged more comfortable than ever following its latest facelift. Some rooms are small, but public areas are pleasant and clubby, and the Cambridge Common location is enchanting. ◈ *16 Garden St, Cambridge, 02138 • Map B1 • 617 547 4800 • www.sheratoncommander. com • $$$*

7 Harvard Square
This nicely renovated former motor inn is, indeed, right on Harvard Square. The tiny lobby has one computer for those who need Internet access, and Wi-Fi is also available. Rooms are tasteful. ◈ *110 Mt Auburn St, Cambridge, 02138 • Map B2 • 617 864 5200 • www. harvardsquarehotel.com • $$*

8 Courtyard Boston Tremont Hotel
At the edge of the Theater District, this 1920s tower hotel underwent restoration that gave fresh glitter to its dramatic public spaces (think crystal chandeliers and marble columns). Rooms are small but modern with first-rate amenities. There are conference rooms for business travelers. ◈ *275 Tremont St, 02116 • Map N5 • 617 426 1400 • www.marriott.com • $$$*

9 Charlesmark
Set in an 1892 Back Bay townhouse, the 40 rooms of this boutique hotel feature custom-made furniture, light-toned woodwork, and Italian tiles. Breakfast is included in the astonishingly low (for the area) rates. ◈ *655 Boylston St, 02116 • Map L5 • 617 247 1212 • www.charlesmark hotel.com • $$*

10 Inn at St Botolph
Great for a romantic getaway, this boutique hotel near Symphony Hall boasts the finest contemporary design. Its red-brick townhouse exterior looks like a private home. The sunny rooms have queen-size beds. ◈ *99 St Botolph St, 02116 • Map E3 • 617 236 8099 • www. innatstbotolph.com • $$$*

Left **Isaac Harding House** Right **Bertram Inn**

🔟 Budget B&Bs

1 Isaac Harding House
Situated in a quiet Cambridge neighborhood, this 1860s Victorian home is now a popular B&B. The 14 guest rooms are spacious and bright. High-speed Internet connections are available in public rooms. 🔹 *288 Harvard St, Cambridge 02139 • Map C2 • 617 876 2888 • www.cambridge inns.com • $$*

2 Beech Tree Inn
Most rooms in this friendly Victorian-style B&B have private baths. Guests also have use of a parlor. 🔹 *83 Longwood Ave, Brookline, 02446 • 617 277 1620 • www.thebeech treeinn.com • No DA • $$*

3 Oasis Guest House
Close to Berklee School of Music, the Hynes Convention Center, and Symphony Hall, Oasis has rooms in a townhouse on a quiet one-way street a little removed from the hubbub of Massachusetts Avenue. Guests share a small outdoor deck. 🔹 *22 Edgerly Rd, 02115 • 617 267 2262 • www.oasisgh.com • $$*

4 Bertram Inn
In a quiet residential neighborhood, this B&B began life as a private home built in the Tudor Revival style. It only has 10 rooms and four small suites, all tastefully decorated with styles varying between Arts & Crafts, late Victorian, and just downright eclectic. 🔹 *92 Sewall Ave, Brookline, 02446 • 617 566 2234 • www.bertraminn.com • No DA • $$*

5 Irving House
An older rooming house turned B&B, Irving House is tucked away in a leafy neighborhood next to Harvard University. Rooms vary from tiny to spacious and some share bathrooms. 🔹 *24 Irving St, Cambridge, 02138 • Map C1 • 617 547 4600 • www. cambridgeinns.com • $$*

6 John Jeffries House
This former nurse's quarters now serves as a pleasant 46-room inn. Public areas sport the Neo-Federal look; guest rooms are bare but cheerful; and most have kitchenettes. 🔹 *14 David G. Mugar Way, 02114 • Map M2 • 617 367 1866 • www.johnjeffries house.com • $$*

7 Newbury Guest House
Several Back Bay residences have been linked inside to create this homey 32-room guest house. Rooms vary in size, but tend to be cozy with eclectic furnishings. Good value for the location. 🔹 *261 Newbury St, 02116 • Map K5 • 617 670 6000 • www.newbury guesthouse.com • $$*

8 Beacon Inn
Two 19th-century brownstone buildings, about a mile (0.6 km) apart, are located in residential Brookline neighborhoods on the "T" Green Line, offering easy access to all Boston's attractions. Both feature carved wooden trim, high ceilings, and full breakfast. 🔹 *1087 & 1750 Beacon St, 02146 • Map B5 • 617 566 0088 • www.beaconinn.com • No DA • $$*

9 A Friendly Inn at Harvard
This large 17-room Queen Anne-style house is steps from Harvard Square and the Harvard University museums. The great location, gracious hospitality, and modern facilities, such as Internet access, make this a very popular hotel, particularly with visiting scholars and prospective students. 🔹 *1673 Cambridge St, 02138 • Map C1 • 617 547 7851 • www.afinow.com • $$*

10 Constitution Inn
This 147-room facility in Charlestown Navy Yard serves military personnel, but welcomes all. The rooms here are clean and modern, and guests can use the well-equipped fitness center with pool and sauna free of charge. 🔹 *150 3rd Ave, Charlestown Navy Yard, Charlestown, 02129 • Map G2 • 617 241 8400 • www. constitutioninn.org • $$*

The best li'l guesthouse in Cambridge
Harding House

Streetsmart

Note: *Unless otherwise stated, all hotels accept credit cards and have en-suite bathrooms and air conditioning*

Price Categories

For a standard, double room per night (with breakfast if included), taxes, and extra charges.

$	under $150
$$	$150–$250
$$$	$250–$350
$$$$	$350–$450
$$$$$	over $450

Left **Midtown**

🔟 Budget Hotels & Inns

1 Hotel Tria
Situated near Alewife "T" station at the edge of Cambridge, the chic style and distinct comfort of Tria suggest luxury, however the prices are definitely in the budget range. ◈ 220 Alewife Brook Pkwy, Cambridge, 02138 • 617 491 8000 • www.hoteltria.com • $$

2 La Quinta Inn and Suites
This motor inn is a five-minute drive from downtown Boston and offers an airport shuttle service. Spacious rooms and suites have tasteful decor and include dual phone lines, 50-channel cable TV, and high-speed Internet connections. ◈ 23 Cummings St, Somerville, 02145 • 617 625 5300 • www.lq.com • $$

3 Chandler Inn
A popular choice for business travelers on a budget, this 55-room hotel in the South End is a short walk from Back Bay "T". Rooms are simple and comfy with TVs and phones with voice mail. ◈ 26 Chandler St, 02116 • Map M6 • 617 482 3450 • www.chandler inn.com • No DA • $$

4 Boston Common Hotel
One of the best-kept secrets of Back Bay, this once-private club has cozy but comfortable rooms at relatively bargain rates. Some single rooms are available. There are good discounts to be had in slow season. ◈ 40 Trinity Pl, 02116 • Map F5 • 617 933 7700 • www. bostoncommonhotel.com • $$

5 Inn at Longwood Medical Center
This Best Western affiliate is an attractive and comfortable 144-room hotel in the Longwood Medical Area. It caters principally to families of patients but is open to all travelers. ◈ 342 Longwood Ave, 02115 • 617 731 4700 • www. bestwestern.com • $$

6 Midtown
This 159-room budget motor inn in Back Bay was built in the 1960s but has been extensively renovated to bring it up-to-date. Kids appreciate the outdoor pool and drivers enjoy the significant bonus of secure parking. ◈ 220 Huntington Ave, 02115 • Map E5 • 617 262 1000 • www.midtown hotel.com • $$

7 Hotel 140
Located literally just around the corner from the Back Bay Amtrak station, this budget hotel has refurbished the rooms of the country's first YMCA into minimalist examples of how to use small spaces. ◈ 140 Clarendon St, 02116 • Map F5 • 617 585 5600 • www. hotel140.com • $$

8 College Club
This private club devoted to promoting higher education also has 11 guest rooms available in its sophisticated Back Bay townhouse. Several smaller rooms share baths (only adequate for singles). ◈ 44 Commonwealth Ave, 02116 • Map L4 • 617 536 9510 • No DA • $$-$$$

9 Hampton Inn
This 114-room chain hotel features high-speed Internet service in all rooms as well as underground parking for no additional fee. Rooms are modest but include a good desk area, making the hotel popular with business folk on a budget. ◈ 191 Monsignor O'Brien Hwy, Cambridge, 02141 • 617 494 5300 • www.hamptoninn.com • $$-$$$

10 Holiday Inn Express
Travelers hunting for a clean and dependable roadside lodging close to Boston need look no further. This eight-floor building has 112 rooms designed for short-term business stays – the rooms have good work areas. Limited free parking available. It's a short walk to Lechmere "T" stop. ◈ 250 Monsignor O'Brien Hwy, Cambridge, 02141 • Map F2 • 617 577 7600 • www.hiecambridge. com • $$

General Index

Acknowledgements

The Authors

Patricia Harris and David Lyon write about travel, food, fine arts, and popular culture for many publications including *Boston Magazine*, *Boston Globe*, *Yankee*, *Robb Report*, and *hungrytravelers.com*. They also co-wrote the Dorling Kindersley *Eyewitness Travel Guide to Boston*.

Jonathan Schultz is a travel writer based in Portland, Maine. He has contributed extensive local content to *Boston Magazine*, Boston.citysearch. com; LosAngeles.citysearch.com; as well as having compiled a guide to Boston for Z Publishing.

Produced by
Departure Lounge, London

Editorial Directors
Georgina Matthews, Ella Milroy

Art Director Lisa Kosky

Picture Researcher Naomi Peck

Editorial & Design Assistants
Alexandra Hajok, Sarah Billyard, Trond Wilhelmsen

Proofreader Stephanie Driver

Indexer Hilary Bird

Fact Checker Jillian Dudek

Photographer John Coletti

Additional Photography
Demetrio Carrasco, Patricia Harris, David Lyon, Ella Milroy, Linda Whitwam

Illustrators Lee Redmond

Maps Dominic Beddow, Simonetta Giori (Draughtsman Ltd, London)

AT DORLING KINDERSLEY
Senior Art Editor Marisa Renzullo

Publishing Manager Helen Townsend

Publisher Douglas Amrine

Senior Cartographic Editor
Casper Morris

Senior DTP Designer Jason Little

Production Controller
Melanie Dowland

Revisions Team
Emer FitzGerald, Fay Franklin, Anna Freiberger, Jo Gardner, Integrated Publishing Solutions, Claire Jones, Priya Kukadia, Esther Labi, Carly Madden, Nicola Malone, Sam Merrell, Mani Ramaswamy, Ellen Root, Susana Smith, Karen Villabona, Ros Walford, Hugo Wilkinson

RESTAURANT: 40tr; THE ESTATE BOSTON: 51tr. FAIRMONT BATTERY WHARF: 147tl; FAIRMONT COPLEY PLAZA: 46tr; THE FELT CLUB: 102tl; FRANKLIN PARK ZOO: 60t; 126tl. GETTY IMAGES: Steve Dunwell 98tl; GIBSON HOUSE: 21cr; 83c; GREATER BOSTON CONVENTION & VISITORS' BUREAU: 6t; 55tr; 80tr; 113b. PATRICIA HARRIS & DAVID LYON: 110tl; HARRISON GRAY OTIS HOUSE: 76tl; HARVARD UNIVERSITY ART MUSEUMS © President and Fellows of Harvard College: 17bl, Busch-Reisinger Museum/ Katya Kallsen 17cr; HULTON GETTY: 18tl; 18tr; 38tr; 38tl. ISABELLA STEWART GARDNER MUSEUM 2002: 7cr; 28tl; 28c; 28b; 28–29c; 29tl; 29tr; 29br. JAMES LEMASS: 4–5; 34–5; 53tr; 54tl; 55b; 68tl; 68tr; 68b; 70tl; 70tr; 93tl; 100–01; JOHNNY D'S: 48tl; JORDAN HALL: 112tr (Nick Wheeler). LANGHAM BOSTON HOTEL: Robert Wesley Rollend 102tr; LEKKER HOME: 108tr; LEONARDO MEDIABANK: 146tl. MARY EVANS PICTURE LIBRARY: 36t; 37r; 38c; 39r; MASSACHUSETTS BAY TRANSPORT-ATION AUTHORITY: backflap; MASSACHUSETTS COLLEGE OF ART 115tl; MASSACHUSETTS STATE HOUSE: 2c; 6tr; 8tr; 11cl; 11b; 75tr; MIT LIST VISUAL ARTS CENTER: 120b (*Amoreles vs Amorales* by

Carlos Amorales, 2002); MUSEUM OF FINE ARTS: 3bl; 7tl; 22b; 22tl; 22–23c; 23tl; 23c; 23b; 24tl; 24tr; 24bl; 25t; 25c; MUSEUM OF SCIENCE: 60cb; 61tr; 118tr; 121tl. NEWBURY COMICS: 85tl; NICHOLS HOUSE MUSEUM: 75bl NIELSEN GALLERY: 84tl (*Summer Incoming Tide I* by John Walker, 2001 oil on linen); NEW ENGLAND AQUARIUM: 7br; 90tr; 32tl; 32b; 32–33c; 33tl; 33b. OLD NORTH CHURCH © Old North Church: 9cb; 10c; 90cr; 91c; 93tr; OLD STATE HOUSE frontflap; 97tr. POWER-STOCK: 70b. RADIUS: 41tr (Keller & Keller); REGATTABAR: 124tl. SCULLERS JAZZ CLUB: 48bl; SUMMER SHACK: 43tr. TAVOLO: 131tl; TRINITY CHURCH: frontflap; 7tr; 26bc, 26–7c,7tr (Jim Scherer); 27tr, 27cr (Peter Vanderwarker); 27bl (Trinity Church archives). UPSTAIRS ON THE SQUARE: 40tl; USS CONSTITUTION MUSEUM, BOSTON: 31t (Janet Stearns). VENU: 109tr. WHEELOCK FAMILY THEATRE: 139tr

The publishers would like to thank all other churches, museums, hotels, restaurants, shops, galleries, clubs and nights that have also supplied images but are too numerous to thank individually. All other images are © Dorling Kindersley. For further information see *www.dkimages.com*

Special Editions of DK Travel Guides

DK Travel Guides can be purchased in bulk quantities at discounted prices for use in promotions or as premiums. We are also able to offer special editions and personalized jackets, corporate imprints, and excerpts from all of our books, tailored specifically to meet your own needs.

To find out more, please contact:

(in the United States)
specialsales@dk.com

(in the UK) **travelspecialsales@uk.dk.com**

(in Canada) DK Special Sales at
general@tourmaline.ca

(in Australia) **business.development@pearson.com.au**

Selected Street Index